ACADEMIC ADVISING:
The Key to Student Success
Edited by Terry O'Banion

ACADEMIC ADVISING:
The Key to Student Success
Edited by Terry O'Banion

Community College Press®
A division of the American Association of Community Colleges
Washington, DC

Suggested citation:

O'Banion, T. (Ed.). (2013). *Academic advising: The key to student success.* Washington, DC: Community College Press.

Community College Press® is a division of the American Association of Community Colleges (AACC), the primary advocacy organization for the nation's community colleges. The association represents more than 1,200 two-year, associate degree–granting institutions and more than 13 million students. AACC promotes community colleges through five strategic action areas: recognition and advocacy for community colleges; student access, learning, and success; community college leadership development; economic and workforce development; and global and intercultural education. Information about AACC and community colleges may be found at www.aacc.nche.edu.

Design: Gratzer Graphics LLC
Printing: Global Printing

ISBN 978-0-87117-397-3

Printed in the United States of America.
First Edition, First Printing

Contents

FOREWORD

Walter G. Bumphus

T HE GROWING FOCUS ON COLLEGE completion among policymakers, academicians, and leading foundations has also brought renewed examination of the elements that foster student success. In his recently published work, *Completing College: Rethinking Institutional Action*, Vincent Tinto (2012), considered one of the preeminent scholars on student retention, identified four critical "conditions" that promote student success and thus lead to higher completion rates: expectations, support, assessment and feedback, and involvement.

Related to assessment, Tinto wrote, "Students are more likely to succeed in institutions that assess their performance and provide frequent feedback in ways that enable students, faculty, and staff alike to adjust their behaviors to better promote student success." I couldn't agree more. The first 18 years of my 30-year career in higher education were spent as a dean of students and then vice president of student affairs. I have seen personally the need for, importance of, and outcomes from having a consistent and well-planned advising program. Believe me, there is no more humbling experience than knowing that the guidance you provide a student, to a significant degree, will help to determine how well that student succeeds on campus and, ultimately, in the world of work. Thus, I could not have been more enthusiastic to see another preeminent scholar, Terry O'Banion, who pioneered one of the early models in student advising at community colleges, take up that mantle once again with this current work. He has done so with a passion uniquely his own and with an intellect that has led innovation for decades.

I can speak to Terry's earlier work firsthand. First at East Arkansas Community College and then at Howard Community College (MD) in the late 1970s and early 1980s, I used the original O'Banion model of academic advising to implement what I found to be highly effective advising programs. It provided the appropriate student-centered approach—one that I believe was a precursor for today's expanded focus on student success. The validity of that approach and the heightened need for solid, structured, and sequential academic advising is just as relevant today. When I speak with my daughter Fran Maynard, who serves as North Lake College's (TX) dean of student success and has responsibility for academic advising there, she underscores the fundamental importance of this need.

At state and national levels, recognition of the importance of better student supports and integrated advising programs is clear. California is currently moving forward with the Student Success Act of 2012, which will require that campuses participate in a common assessment system and post a student success campus score as a condition of funding. The final report of the 21st-Century Commission on the Future of Community Colleges, sponsored by the American Association of Community Colleges (AACC), included several recommendations that address the importance of increasing the numbers of students completing certificates and degrees through better student support and aligning courses of study to workplace requirements.

Academic Advising: The Key to Student Success provides contemporary analysis of five successful advising models at community colleges today, highlighting a variety of innovative methods from "LifeMaps" to online advising to peer advising. The models were selected by the two AACC Affiliated Councils comprising advising professionals for the field: the National Council of Instructional Administrators and the National Council on Student Development. We are indebted to both of these organizations for their commitment to developing leadership and organizational structures to support student success.

Terry O'Banion's new research and thoughtful analysis could be neither more timely nor more urgent. Contributing to greater student success and, from there, to higher completion rates, speaks to the core mission of community colleges and to the future of our nation. Over a long and distinguished career, he has been in the vanguard as a thought leader and a scholar. This work provides yet another vitally important resource for our colleges. And, for our students, it may prove to be his most lasting legacy.

Walter G. Bumphus
President and CEO
American Association of Community Colleges

REFERENCES

Tinto, V. (2012). *Completing college: Rethinking institutional action.* Chicago, IL: University of Chicago Press.

PREFACE

Review Panel for *Academic Advising: The Key to Student Success*

National Council of Instructional Administrators

- ◆ Judy Marwick, Provost, Harper College, Palatine, IL

- ◆ Lisa Stich, Vice President, Academics and Student Services, West Shore Community College, Scottville, MI

- ◆ Carl McDonald, Vice President for Academic Affairs, South Georgia College, Douglas, GA

- ◆ Linda Uzureau, Executive Director, NCIA, and Assistant to the President for Community College Partnerships, Governors State University, University Park, IL

National Council on Student Development

- ◆ Ken Ray, Vice President, Student Services and Enrollment Management, Hillsborough Community College, Tampa, FL

- ◆ Kori Bieber, Vice President, Student Services, Rogue Community College, Grants Pass, OR

- ◆ L. Marshall Washington, Campus Vice President, Harrisburg Area Community College, Lancaster, PA

- ◆ Daniel Herbst, Dean, Student Affairs, Chandler-Gilbert Community College, Chandler, AZ

I BEGAN MY CAREER IN COMMUNITY colleges in 1960 as a very young dean of students at Central Florida Junior College in Ocala, Florida. Among all the student services we provided to our students, academic advising loomed as the most formidable challenge. After all, it was the one service we needed to provide to every student every term, and it was the prelude to classroom instruction. Our faculty colleagues could judge how well we did our job by how well students were prepared to begin their educational journey in the classroom.

All our student services staff were quite young and inexperienced, and we did not know very much about student services in general and even less about academic advising in particular. Early on we were strongly influenced by one of the few resources available, *The Faculty in College Counseling* (1959), recognized nationally as the last word on the subject. The author, Melveen Hardee, believed that faculty members were the primary providers of academic advising, and, with no alternative voices to suggest otherwise, we subscribed to her beliefs. We did understand the importance of securing students' feedback about their satisfaction with services so we created an evaluation system and began to assess our experiments.

In our first year we used all faculty as academic advisors. In the second year, based on student evaluations, we used only faculty who were interested in advising and who agreed to participate in training as advisors. In year three we changed systems again and used only professional counselors to do the advising. In our evaluations, students expressed no more satisfaction with one model than another, so in the fourth year we allowed students to self-advise or see a counselor or faculty member of their choice. Once again, student satisfaction did not differ from any of the other surveys of the various models.

These outcomes puzzled me and led me to becoming a student of academic advising as my professional entrée into the world of student development. Later, I conducted the first national study of academic advising in the community college and made my first professional speeches on this topic. If who did advising made little difference to students, then what was the question? I soon figured out that the more important questions were "What is academic advising?" And "What skills, knowledge, and attitudes are required by those who do the advising?"

With this new perspective, I began constructing and testing what emerged as the five steps that make up the process of academic advising in my model:

exploration of life goals, exploration of vocational goals, program choice, course choice, and course scheduling. I went a step further and suggested the skills, knowledge, and attitudes that advisors need to become effective academic advisors regardless of whether they are faculty, counselors, advising specialists, or students. "An Academic Advising Model" first appeared in the *Junior College Journal* in 1972.

In my experience the two questions I focused on in the model were very basic and simple, and I was surprised how the answers in a model I developed struck a chord in the field and would be recognized in 1994 as one of two classic models by the National Academic Advising Association. American College Testing labeled the model as the "O'Banion model of academic advising," and today, if one Googles that reference, there are 11,600 links.

ACADEMIC ADVISING: THE KEY TO STUDENT SUCCESS

The overarching mission of the community college today is student success, sometimes expressed as the completion agenda. They are one and the same except that the completion agenda comes with more sharply focused goals to double by 2020 the number of students who complete 1-year certificates, associate degrees, or who transfer to a 4-year college or university. Never in community college history has such a goal been embraced by so many stakeholders from the White House to the state house and to hundreds of community colleges. Never in the history of the community college has such a goal had so much financial support from philanthropic organizations; the Bill & Melinda Gates Foundation alone has allocated one-half billion dollars to this effort.

As community colleges experiment with and engage in promising and high-impact practices to improve and expand the student success pathway to completion, academic advising is emerging as one of the most important programs in a student's experience. As stated in the original model that frames this monograph, "The purpose of academic advising is to help students select a program of study to meet their life and vocational goals. As such, academic advising is a central and important activity in the process of education. Academic advising occurs at least once each term for every student in the college; few student support functions occur as often or affect so many students." It is not too much to claim academic advising as "the key to student success."

This monograph includes an updated version of the original model published in 1972. It also includes a special chapter by Angela Oriano, who uses rich data on academic advising reflected in numerous studies by the Center for Community College Student Engagement. Most importantly, the monograph includes five chapters by leading specialists in academic advising whose programs have been judged by a national panel as among the most outstanding or exemplary academic advising programs in the country. My contributors and I are pleased to share these models with you and hope they will be useful in designing and redesigning academic advising programs to better ensure the success of our students.

SELECTION PROCESS

In fall 2011, I proposed to the American Association of Community Colleges (AACC) a project to identify outstanding community college academic advising programs to be incorporated in a monograph on academic advising. Walter G. Bumphus and Norma Kent at AACC were very supportive of the proposal and agreed to publish the final product. They were also very helpful in making connections for me with the National Council of Instructional Administrators (NCIA) and the National Council on Student Development (NCSD); both organizations have been full partners in the project.

Linda Uzureau (assistant to the president for community college partnerships, Governors State University, IL, and executive director of NCIA), Marshall Washington (campus vice president, Harrisburg Area Community College, PA, and then-chair of NCSD), and Al Buyok (dean of instruction/chief academic officer, Treasure Valley Community College, OR, and then-chair of NCIA), served with me on the planning committee for this project.

AACC included an invitation in two editions of its newsletter for leaders to nominate academic advising programs considered exemplary or outstanding. The newsletter is sent to 13,000 leaders, including presidents of all community colleges holding membership in the association. NCSD and NCIA each sent a special e-mail to their members inviting them to nominate academic advising programs considered exemplary or outstanding. Invitations were sent to 225 members of NCSD and 465 members of NCIA. In addition, several states and several other organizations sent invitations to leaders inviting them to nominate programs.

It was quite surprising that despite this widespread coverage, there were only 27 programs representing 18 states nominated as exemplary or outstanding. In a conference call with the members of the national panel, it was suggested that this lack of nominations might be an indication of the low quality of academic advising programs in community colleges. Other panel members suggested that it might be an indication of this moment in time in the community college in which there is a great deal of emphasis through Achieving the Dream and the completion agenda on restructuring programs to improve and enhance student success; maybe colleges are in the middle of reforming their academic advising programs and are not quite ready to champion them as exemplary or outstanding.

Once nominated, college contacts provided by the nominees were asked to submit a two-page profile of their academic advising program. The profile included a description of the program and evidence that supported the program as exemplary or outstanding. Eighteen profiles were submitted for consideration. The national panel selected five colleges to invite to submit chapters.

The review panel (see page xiv) included four members each from NCSD and NCIA. Panel members had 3 weeks to review the profiles and identify the programs to be invited to submit chapters for the monograph. I joined panel members in making the final decisions in a conference call on April 9, 2012, and college contacts were notified immediately. We asked the contacts to create their chapters following a set of detailed guidelines that had been vetted by a select group of national leaders in academic advising. We hope the five colleges' stories serve as models that other community colleges will follow to ensure their own students' success.

Terry O'Banion
President Emeritus, League for Innovation in the Community College
Chair, Graduate Faculty, National American University

REFERENCES

Hardee, M. D. (1959). *The faculty in college counseling*. New York, NY: McGraw-Hill.

CHAPTER 1

An Academic Advising Model for the 21st Century

Terry O'Banion

This is the 40th anniversary of Terry O'Banion's seminal article on a model of academic advising that was published by the American Association of Community Colleges in the *Junior College Journal* in 1972. The model has been adapted by hundreds of community colleges and universities in the last four decades and was recognized by the National Academic Advising Association in 1994 as one of two "classics in the literature of academic advising and one of the most cited in the literature." This chapter is an updated version of the original article.

ACADEMIC ADVISING IS THE SECOND most important function in the community college. If it is not conducted with the utmost efficiency and effectiveness, the most important function in the college—instruction— will fail to achieve its purpose of ensuring that students succeed in navigating the curriculum to completion. The purpose of academic advising is to help students select a program of study to meet their life and vocational goals. As such, academic advising is a central and important activity in the process of education.

Academic advising occurs at least once each term for every student in the college; few student support functions occur as often or affect so many students. But while there is general agreement concerning the importance of academic advising for the efficient functioning of the institution and the effective functioning of the student, there is little agreement regarding the nature of academic advising and who should perform the function. The model proposed here defines the process of academic advising and outlines the skills and knowledge required of academic advisors who work with students through this process. It is a flexible model that can be adapted to the needs, resources, and culture of any institution of higher education. Any well-conceived program of academic advising will include activities related to each of the five steps. It may be possible for each of these steps to be explored in a single day; most colleges, however, are likely to consider the process of academic advising as continuous, beginning before the student attends class and continuing throughout the student's stay at the college.

THE FIVE-STEP PROCESS

The process of academic advising includes the following steps: (1) exploration of life goals, (2) exploration of vocational goals, (3) program choice, (4) course choice, and (5) course scheduling. This is, of course, an ideal sequence of steps that moves a student through complex and significant explorations regarding key issues and goals to decisions about which courses to take and when to take them. Too often, colleges fail to connect this sequence for students; too often colleges give short shrift to the first two steps because of the pressing need to address the last three steps. If a college wants to improve the opportunities for student success—in a student's first term and through completion—the student must experience all five steps of the academic advising process.

Step 1: Exploration of Life Goals

A sound and substantive college education should be a life-changing experience for students. In our haste to enroll students and move them to completion, we often fail to acknowledge the value and impact of our own experiences in college that opened up new worlds. We sometimes forget that college is a place for exploring new ideas, making new connections, giving up worn-out views. Students who are first-generation college students from lower socioeconomic backgrounds may have no other place than college for this exploration. A college education should ensure that every student has an opportunity to examine the questions, "Who am I? Where am I going? What difference does it make?" Few students come to us with any experience in exploring these essential questions. Such experiences provide a foundation for clarifying values and creating a satisfying philosophy of life—goals that were basic to the general education programs of the 1950s and 1960s.

The entire college experience and the entire college curriculum should be laced with these questions to provide any depth for the answers, but the exploration should begin as soon as a student first connects with the college. And the exploration must be a major feature of the academic advising process because that is the only function in which every student participates. Furthermore, the process of academic advising is incomplete unless the student has an opportunity to explore life goals as a prelude to exploring vocational goals.

College leaders recognize the importance of students exploring their life goals, and many programs and practices have been designed to provide this experience. In former decades, colleges created classic general education programs that included a personal development course as the heart of the program. In the late 1960s and 1970s at Santa Fe Community College in Gainesville, Florida, the 3-hour course, "The Individual in a Changing Society," was required of every entering student. Many colleges offered courses based on the "Human Potential Seminar" or on encounter groups.

Today the first-year experience and the student success course are the contemporary attempts to help students explore their life goals. In many of these courses, academic advising—along with assessment, orientation, career counseling, and registration—is folded into the experience to better connect the overarching life goal questions with the immediate questions of which courses to take this term. While a course focused on life goals and questions provides more depth and time for students, courses come after the first sessions of academic advising. If students are to benefit by this model of academic advising, then opportunities to explore life goals must be part of the process before students begin their course work. Such explorations should be more affective than intellectual. The following are promising practices colleges might wish to consider.

- As soon as new students connect to the college and begin the admissions process, a special letter from the president or a key vice president should be sent, welcoming the student to a college that provides a life-changing experience. As part of that experience, students are required or urged to read a provocative book or article that comes with a few questions to stimulate discussions that will occur in the required orientation sessions. The book might be provided free by the college, supported by donations from an area business.

- A similar opportunity for students to read and discuss life goal issues could be created using technology in which each student would be required to work through a series of carefully crafted questions leading to an exploration of careers and vocational goals. Students would be required to complete this sequence before they meet with an academic advisor and before they can register. If some of these experiences were explored in a college chat room, opportunities for networking could be created that would help students begin to make connections with other students before they even met on campus.

- At a minimum, students should have an opportunity in advising or orientation sessions to explore some aspects of the essential questions about how they want to live their lives and the role college can play in that process.

Step 2: Exploration of Vocational Goals

Vocational goals are life goals extended into the world of work. What a person is and wants to be (life goals) determines in great part how that person will earn a living and contribute to the general welfare of others (vocational goals). The relationship between life goals and vocational goals is intricate and complex; educators are understandably challenged in their attempts to help students make decisions in these areas. But just because it is a difficult and often time-consuming process in education is no reason to avoid it. Many programs of academic advising flounder because they begin at step three with program choice. It is assumed that students have already made choices regarding life goals and vocational goals when they enter the college—a questionable assumption for college students in general and a harmful and incorrect assumption for community college students in particular.

Although this model of the process of academic advising separates the exploration of life goals from the exploration of vocational goals for the sake of illustration, the two steps cannot and should not be separated when applied to students. It is certainly possible to separate the exploration of life goals into a series of experiences that stand alone, but here we are focusing on a process of academic advising that depends on a connection between the two. Clarifying life goals—as much as they can be clarified at this stage in a student's life—is essential in clarifying vocational goals. In addition to student success courses and first-year experiences, many colleges provide career assessment and career counseling opportunities for students to explore vocational goals. Although they occur after students have completed their first academic advising sessions, service learning experiences can be framed as significant opportunities for students to explore vocational goals.

As most experienced community college educators know, a very large number of community college students are not prepared to make decisions about vocational goals when they enter college. Once these students are clearly identified, they should be required to enroll in a prescribed program for "undecided students." If the college has a classic core of general education courses, this becomes the prescribed program. As an alternative, a learning community that includes a student success course, an introduction to psychology, and a developmental or college-level writing course—or some appropriate cluster of courses—becomes the prescribed program. If the undecided student is enrolling in only one course, that course should be a student success course or an experience in which the exploration of life and vocational goals forms much of the content.

Recent research at the Community College Research Center at Columbia University (Scott-Clayton, 2011) suggests that community colleges offer too many options for students—especially for underprepared, first-generation college students—which may contribute to the low rates of student success. The research confirms that community college students will be more likely to persist and succeed in programs characterized by higher levels of "instructional program coherence"—programs that are tightly and consciously structured like the prescribed program clusters noted in the preceding paragraph.

Step 3: Program Choice

Once the college has provided an opportunity for life and vocational goal exploration through summer advising groups, occupational seminars, orientation programs, self-development classes, programmed guides, technology aides, experiential sessions, etc., the student is ready to make a program choice. Even in a college or university offering traditional programs to a selected clientele, the process of choosing a program is challenging; in a community college offering a comprehensive range of programs to a great diversity of students, the process of choosing a program staggers the imagination. That is why requiring a prescribed and limited program for undecided students makes so much sense.

For students who are sure or have some idea of the program they want to pursue, the decision of a particular program should emerge as part of the exploration of vocational goals. If students are absolutely sure of their choice of program, the academic advising process should move them efficiently and smoothly to the next steps. These students might be channeled to specific programs or departments such as nursing or criminal justice, where faculty advisors help them confirm their choices and in which they are oriented to careers in these areas.

As noted, for students who are undecided about a choice of programs, the college should prescribe a limited program. For students who are a bit unsure but who have inclinations toward a program, the advising process must help them design a program that will help them test out their interests and offer options for changing their minds without losing credit. This is tricky business for the student and the advisor; the most effective advisors are required for this stage in the process.

Step 4: Course Choice

Once the program is selected, students choose courses for the immediate term and perhaps for subsequent terms. Most colleges provide program guides that list the required courses, often noting the courses required by different transfer institutions. It is important to note prerequisites in selecting courses and to make sure students possess the competencies required for the courses. For students who are unprepared for college-level courses, advisors must be particularly sensitive in helping students understand the need for developmental courses and selecting a sequence that will lead to success.

In selecting specific courses for a term, there are many challenges that require knowledge and training on the part of personnel who assist in this process. Students who register late will not have as many choices as those who register early. Low-income and poorly prepared students tend to register later than other students, and they will be frustrated and disappointed when required or recommended courses are closed or not available at the preferred times.

Colleges committed to the completion agenda and the student success pathway will require students to create personal development plans or road maps that can frame their choices and track progress as they navigate through the college. The plans and maps will include the required and elective courses for the program the student has chosen and must be accurate. They will also reflect course credits transferred from other institutions. So the choice of courses for a term is not a simple process, and since advisors often sign off on these plans, this is a significant step in the academic advising process.

Step 5: Course Scheduling

Selecting the times courses are to be taken is often thought to be a simple task. But many community college students are unfamiliar with such concepts as semester-hour credit, transfer, GPA, developmental studies, etc. They are often left on their own to figure out a schedule of classes to attend 3 days a week rather than the 5 to which they were accustomed in high school. While the scheduling of courses may appear easy to professional educators who themselves have registered and scheduled courses many times in their collegiate experiences, it can be a challenging experience to the nontraditional student who attends community college.

In 2007–2008, nearly 84% of community college students worked while attending college; 42.9% worked full-time jobs while 40.7% worked part-time jobs (Staklis & Chen, 2010). Determining the times to schedule their courses is a particularly daunting task for this majority of students. Many students are limited by the times they can take courses because they have family responsibilities, must arrange schedules around child care, and depend on other sources for transportation.

THE ELEMENTS OF EFFECTIVE ADVISING

The Characteristics of Effective Advisors

To better understand the nature of the process of academic advising, it is important to consider the skills, knowledge, and attitudes required of the personnel who will assist students in each of the steps, which are described in Table 1.1. In addition to these requirements, all personnel who contribute to the process of academic advising must understand how to apply the technology used to undergird these five steps.

A Team Approach

Although systems of academic advising have been designed as "faculty advising" systems or "counselor-based" systems in the past, this model strongly supports academic advising as an institution-wide team approach. Academic advising is too important in the student success pathway to assign it to only one group in the institution. Personnel should be assigned to the process in terms of their skills, knowledge, and attitudes required for each of the five steps. Students, counselors, instructors, and special personnel such as student assistants,

Table 1.1 ◆ The Skills, Knowledge, and Attitudes of Effective Academic Advisors Throughout the Five-Step Process

Step 1: Exploration of Life Goals	
Knowledge • Student characteristics and development. • Decision-making processes. • Psychology and sociology.	*Attitudes* • Appreciation of individual differences. • Belief in worth and dignity of all students. • Belief that all students have potential.
Skills • Counseling techniques.	

Step 2: Exploration of Vocational Goals	
Knowledge • Student characteristics and development. • Decision-making processes. • Psychology and sociology. • Vocational fields.	*Attitudes* • Appreciation of individual differences. • Belief in worth and dignity of all students. • Belief that all students have potential. • Understanding of the changing nature of work in society. • Acceptance of all fields of work as worthy and dignified.
Skills • Counseling techniques. • Test interpretation.	

Step 3: Program Choice	
Knowledge • Programs available in the college. • Program requirements (e.g., special entrance requirements, fees, time commitments).	• University requirements for transfer programs. • Performance of others in the program. • Success of those who have completed the program.

Step 4: Course Choice	
Knowledge • Courses available. • Special information (e.g., prerequisites, availability, transferability, graduation requirements, appropriate sequencing for universities). • Rules and regulations (e.g., probation and suspension, academic and work limitations).	• Availability of honors and or developmental courses. • Instructors and their teaching styles. • Student's ability (as indicated by test scores, high school record). • Course content.

Step 5: Course Scheduling	
Knowledge • Course schedules. • System for scheduling and changing schedules. • Work and commuting requirements.	

community volunteers, and advising specialists contribute to the process in terms of their competencies.

The student is responsible for decision making throughout the process. Students must be engaged in academic advising as full partners from the beginning. While the student's role will depend on experience, ability, and clarity of goals, all students should be required to review prepared materials about vocational goals and program choices or to participate in special summer or preenrollment sessions to prepare for making decisions about programs and courses. Academic advising should be mandatory for every student every term, and the student should be prepared to meet his or her obligations.

In the team approach, counselors should have responsibility for helping students explore life and vocational goals. Ideally, such exploration should occur in small personal interactive groups during the summer for new students. A programmed guide designed to help students explore life and vocational goals could be developed if face-to-face groups are not possible. Once students are attending college, there is still a need to offer continuing opportunities for life and vocational goal exploration. Special seminars on occupations, experiential approaches to job sampling, service learning, voluntary encounter groups, learning communities, and student success courses are only a few of the ways in which the college can provide significant opportunities for students to discover meaning in their lives. In addition to this direct involvement with students, counselors should prepare special information for instructors and students to clarify and support their roles in the academic advising process. Counselors should also provide staff development experiences for instructors and student assistants to improve and expand their competencies in academic advising.

The primary role of the instructor in the team approach is to assist students with choosing programs and courses. Assuming the student has explored vocational goals and has selected a program, the student can then be assigned to an instructor in a department or division that reflects the career focus the student wants to explore. Instructors can provide a valuable experiential background for the student who explores a program in which the instructor is a professional. Some departments will provide an orientation to career clusters for groups of students;

others will assign selected instructors to individual students to continue the process of program and course selection; in some colleges where counselors are assigned to departments or divisions, the counselors will orchestrate these sessions.

Few instructors have the time necessary for staff development activities designed to help them become effective advisors. If they teach full loads, participate on committees, and sponsor clubs and organizations, there is little time left for staff development. Unless there is an opportunity for instructors to learn about test interpretation, programs and courses, rules and regulations, transfer requirements, and many other aspects of the academic advising process, they cannot be expected to perform effectively.

If instructors are to participate in the process of academic advising in a professional way, then some important conditions must exist:

- Academic advising must be recognized by the college as an important activity in the life of the institution. This means that instructors are rewarded for their participation, perhaps by recognition of their contributions at the time of evaluation for rank and pay or in reduced class loads.

- There must be a sensible student load. Some national studies have suggested that there be no more than 15 advisees without a reduced teaching assignment.

- There must be a continuing staff development program for all advisors and a special, more intensive program for new instructors before they are allowed to participate.

- There must be special concern for the advisory skills of instructors, which means that only those who qualify should participate.

- There must be an adequate number of professional counselors available to handle referrals and the large number of students who are undecided about life and vocational goals.

- There must be sufficient clerical help available to ensure that instructors have information when they need it and do not perform unnecessary clerical tasks.

- Instructors must guard against using the system to recruit students into courses and programs not of the students' choice.

- ◆ Cooperation and coordination must exist between the instructional program and the student personnel program to ensure the best use of all advising personnel in the best service to students.

- ◆ Finally, there must be a program of evaluation by students, instructors, counselors, and advising specialists in order that sensible modification can be made in a system that is ever changing.

Many colleges, realizing there will never be enough counselors and full-time instructors for the academic advising of the great numbers of students who flock to community colleges, have created academic advising specialists. In some cases the specialists are full-time staff with bachelor's degrees, who are qualified to assist students with all five steps of the advising process; select adjunct faculty could also be trained for this role. Students with a successful history in the college, students who have graduated and are looking for summer work, and community volunteers can be trained to assist with the final step in the process—course scheduling. And some of these students and volunteers can be trained for step four—course choice. Counselors and instructors should seldom be assigned this task, which is an ineffective use of well-paid and overqualified institutional resources.

CONCLUSION

The model of academic advising proposed in this chapter has been adapted by numerous colleges over the last 40 years. The model has two key features that sustain its viability: (1) it defines academic advising as a system of five key steps that every student should navigate; and (2) it outlines the skills, knowledge, and attitudes required of advising personnel for each of the five steps. Based on these two features, the model proposes that academic advising should be designed as an institution-wide team approach utilizing the competencies of counselors, instructors, and advising specialists with the student taking responsibility throughout the process.

Academic advising occurs every term for every student and should be mandatory; it is the prelude to the central activity of the college—instruction. Certainly the college should organize its resources to ensure that this prelude is sufficiently effective so that the student will have the greatest possible opportunity to navigate the student success pathway to completion.

REFERENCES

Scott-Clayton, J. (2011, January). *The shapeless river: Does a lack of structure inhibit students' progress at community colleges?* (CCRC Brief No. 25.) New York: Columbia University Teachers College, Community College Research Center.

Staklis, S., & Chen, X. (2010). *Profile of undergraduate students: Trends from selected years, 1995–1996 to 2007–2008* (NCES 2010-220). Washington, DC: U.S. Department of Education, National Center for Educational Statistics. Retrieved from http://nces.ed.gov/pubs2010/2010220.pdf

CHAPTER 2

Effective Advising: Learning From Students' Experiences

Angela Oriano

Since 2001, the Center for Community College Student Engagement (the Center) has been surveying students to explore their experiences and to learn from them how community colleges might better serve them. In a 2012 publication, *Students Speak: Are We Listening*, Kay M. McClenney, director of the Center, and Arleen Arnsparger, project manager of the Center's Initiative on Student Success, share what they have learned from listening to students through not only surveys but also face-to-face interviews. The following are a few quotes from students about their experience with academic advising.

"After you do your placement testing, you go meet with an advisor to pick out your classes and see what classes you need, but my advisor wasn't really helpful. She kind of said, 'Here are the classes you need and go make your schedule.' I had a whole bunch of questions for her, and said I'd have to come back" (p. 66).

"I think the counselors should be there to be able to tell you not just what the degrees are because I can read in the book what the degree is. What I want to know is what the degree entails, what kind of jobs you can get with that degree" (p. 69).

"Mine [student success course] was a six-week [class], so it ended last week, but it was actually really useful. She gave us a scavenger hunt, and you had to go around, and one group went to financial aid and then presented all the information, and one went to the tutoring center. All the services the school has, that's actually how I kind of learned the most about them was through that class" (p. 79).

"Good advising is one of the key conditions that promotes retention for it reflects an institution's commitment to the education of students."

—Vincent Tinto (1987)

A S THE NATION'S COMMUNITY COLLEGES are gearing up to meet the challenge of America's college completion agenda—to increase completion of postsecondary credentials by 50% over the next decade—they are intentionally focusing attention on their colleges' front doors. Many colleges have begun routine student cohort tracking in an effort to understand where students are lost along the way. Also, institutions are examining intake processes to discern how they can be improved—often discovering that such processes, supported by long-standing institutional policies, hinder rather than foster student success.

Students do their best to navigate complex systems designed mostly for the institution's benefit rather than their own. Some students do not even make it through the initial processes, others drop out before their second academic term, and far fewer students persist in subsequent terms. This reality does not bode well for a nation that must now educate more of its citizens than at any time ever before.

Academic advising is a critical lynchpin for student success. Empirical evidence abounds, although much of it relates to 4-year college students, linking academic advising to student persistence. Research indicates that recurrent and meaningful academic advising, especially when focused on academic or career planning, increases student engagement (Astin, 1984; Pascarella, 1980, 1985; Terenzini, Pascarella, & Lorang, 1982; Tinto, 1987). A large-scale validation study conducted by the Center for Community College Student Engagement (the Center) confirms that the more engaged students are—with faculty, staff, students, and their course work—the more likely they are to learn, persist, and achieve their educational goals (McClenney & Marti, 2006). Every year for the last decade, students responding to the Community College Survey of Student Engagement (CCSSE) have reported that, among an array of student support services, the most important is academic planning and advising. Yet many students also indicated that they did not know about or use the service (CCCSE, 2011).

Given the relationships among academic advising, engagement, and student outcomes, the purpose of this chapter is to describe findings from the Center's student surveys, and to augment those findings by adding student focus group and institutional data that illuminate what students currently are experiencing or not experiencing. Information from the Center will also show the way toward needed improvements in the academic advising process. The chapter is grounded in the conviction—based both on college experience and empirical research—that advising is a fundamental element in college work to strengthen student success.

UNDERSTANDING COMMUNITY COLLEGE STUDENTS

Demographics and Characteristics

The first step in designing processes that work for community college students is to understand the diverse population community colleges serve. In the United States, nearly 1,200 community colleges enroll a total of about 8 million credit students, which constitute 45% of all U.S. undergraduates. Fifty-seven percent of them are women and 43% men. Thirty-nine percent are 21 years of age or younger, 45% are between the ages of 22 and 39, and the average age is 28 (AACC, 2013). Community colleges enroll disproportionately high numbers of students who exhibit certain characteristics that put them statistically at risk of not completing college—for example, those who attend part time, are first-generation college students, did not enter college directly after high school, are single parents, come from low-income families, or are students of color. A snapshot of demographics and employment status is shown in Table 2.1.

These demographic data clearly depict the diverse student population that the nation's public community and technical colleges serve. As Frost (1991) noted, "Because advisers can encourage students to explore their differences as positive factors, the advising relationship can be particularly responsive to pluralism" (p. 1). While the diverse community college student population presents challenges for practitioners seeking to design educational experiences that work for all students, there also are inherent opportunities for building community that benefits society far beyond the walls of the educational institution. There is no doubt that these demographic data also demonstrate the absolute need for colleges to adopt and implement holistic systems of academic advising that take into account not only demographic and cultural differences across the student population, but also the multiple responsibilities students juggle and students' level of academic preparation for college-level work. Simply stated, a well-designed system for academic advising cannot use a one-size-fits-all approach.

In addition to understanding student characteristics, colleges truly focused on helping more students attain their academic goals are obliged to examine institutional culture for evidence of ingrained beliefs about students. Do students bring assets or only deficits with them to college? Are they capable of learning, given the right conditions? Does the college choose to emphasize the student's "right to fail" or the student's right to learn to succeed? In addition to understanding who their students are, and how the institution perceives them, college leaders must also be willing to explore, understand, and use students' lived experiences to inform the design (or redesign) of educational practices.

Students' Experiences

A second important step in innovating systems is to understand the experiences of students—not from the practitioners' perspective, but from the students' perspective. The Center has provided colleges with reliable and actionable data for more than a decade through the administration of a number of national surveys (see Table 2.2, page 21). Built upon empirical research, the Center's two student surveys, CCSSE and the Survey of Entering Student Engagement (SENSE), enable colleges to perform external benchmarking with peer colleges and internal benchmarking among different student subgroups. These survey results

Table 2.1 ◆ Public Community College Student Statistics

Enrolled part time	59%
Enrolled full time	41%
First generation to attend college	40%
Single parents	16%
White	52%
Hispanic	18%
Black	15%
Other/unknown ethnicity	9%
Asian/Pacific Islander	6%
Native American	1%
Full-time students employed full time	21%
Full-time students employed part time	59%
Part-time students employed full time	40%
Part-time students employed part time	47%

Note. From AACC (2013).

are useful in confirming existing perceptions among faculty, staff, and administrators about what their institutions do well and where improvement is needed. Often survey results also challenge existing perceptions, thereby catalyzing campus conversations that help colleges focus their efforts to improve student engagement (McCormick & McClenney, 2012). Frequently, a gap exists between what colleges think they do for and with students and the reality of students' experiences.

CCSSE has been administered to a random sample of more than 1.5 million students—representing a total enrollment of 6.4 million students—at 848 colleges in 49 states plus the District of Columbia, five Canadian provinces, Bermuda, the Marshall Islands, and the Northern Mariana Islands. CCSSE is administered during the spring academic term; thus it generally surveys more experienced (not in their first term) students, gathering information about their overall college experience. The survey focuses on educational practices and student behaviors associated with higher levels of learning, persistence, and completion.

SENSE was launched in 2007. In contrast to CCSSE, which is administered in the spring term and provides a broad picture of student engagement, SENSE is designed to illuminate community college students' earliest experiences. SENSE data yield a focused snapshot of what students encounter from the time of their first contacts with a college through the end of their first 3 weeks of class. The survey focuses on entry and intake processes, including academic assessment and course placement, academic planning and advising, college orientation programs or courses, student success courses, first-year experience programs, early classroom experiences, and academic support. Since the 2008 national field test, a random sample of approximately 162,000 entering students from 273 colleges in 41 states, plus the District of Columbia, Nova Scotia, the Marshall Islands, and Northern Mariana Islands—representing a total credit enrollment of more than 2.2 million students—have participated in SENSE.

Increasingly, community colleges are recognizing the importance of focusing attention and efforts on the front door of the college. The reason for this is simple: Far too many students are lost during their first academic year. National data reflect this reality. Among students who begin in the fall, close to half (46%) will be gone by the subsequent fall term (ACT, 2010). Among the colleges that have participated in the Center's Entering Student Success Institute (ESSI)—nearly 90 colleges from across the nation, diverse in terms of size and populations served—the proportion of students who establish no academic traction in their first term of college is startling. ESSI colleges report that 10%–30% of entering students earned zero credits during their first academic term. According to a 2008 report, only 15% of students who earn no credits in their first term will persist to the second term. By contrast, 74% of students who earn credit in their first fall term will persist to

Table 2.2 ◆ Surveys Administered by the Center for Community College Student Engagement

Survey of Entering Student Engagement (SENSE)

SENSE focuses on students' experiences from the time of their decision to attend college through the end of the first 3 weeks of the fall academic term. The survey assesses practices that are most likely to engage entering students and ensure that they successfully complete the critical first term of college to create pathways for further advancement. SENSE data cited in this chapter are from the 2011 cohort, which consists of slightly more than 94,000 entering students from 217 colleges in 39 states, the District of Columbia, and the Northern Mariana Islands. This chapter also contains data from two special-focus modules. The Academic Advising and Planning special-focus module was administered at 14 colleges in 11 states, yielding responses from more than 6,200 entering students. The Student Success Courses module was administered at 17 colleges in 12 states, yielding approximately 3,300 responses.

Community College Survey of Student Engagement (CCSSE)

CCSSE is administered during the spring academic term; thus, it generally surveys more experienced students (not in their first term) and gathers information about their overall college experience. The survey focuses on educational practices associated with higher levels of learning, persistence, and completion. CCSSE data cited in this chapter are from the 2011 cohort, which includes students from 699 institutions from 48 states and the District of Columbia, five Canadian provinces, Bermuda, and the Northern Mariana Islands.

Community College Faculty Survey of Student Engagement (CCFSSE)

CCFSSE is administered in conjunction with CCSSE to faculty teaching credit courses during the academic term in which the college is participating in the student survey. The survey reports on instructors' perceptions about student experiences, faculty teaching practices, and use of professional time.

Community College Institutional Survey (CCIS)

CCIS is completed by community college practitioners. Developed as part of the Center's initiative on high-impact practices, CCIS produces information about whether and how colleges implement a variety of promising practices. CCIS data cited in this report combine responses from the 2011 pilot and 2012 administrations in which 478 colleges from 45 states, the District of Columbia, Canada, and the Marshall Islands participated.

the spring (Clery &Topper, 2008). Thus, early academic success is consequential, as it is the only available pathway to subsequent success.

The Center's data strongly suggest that, in general, colleges are not systematically engaging students in the kinds of initial academic planning and advising necessary for student success, although they report they are. If, as O'Banion suggests in chapter 1, academic advising is "the second most important function in the college," then student survey findings indicate that our colleges' academic advising systems are failing to earn a passing grade. Among the 478 colleges responding to the Community College Institutional Survey (CCCSE, 2012a), 80% of colleges reported that they require all first-time, full-time students to participate in academic advising, and 50% of colleges reported requiring academic advising for all entering students (full- and part-time). Yet less than a quarter of entering students (23%) said that a specific person was assigned to them so they could see that person each time they needed information or assistance. Perhaps most telling of all is this: 50% of entering students reported that their family and friends are their primary source of academic advising, followed by instructors (26%) and college staff (12%) (CCCSE, 2012c). Thus, no matter how well-designed the system is, nor what theory or model of academic advising the college uses, the harsh reality is that too many students do not know about academic advising—and, even when they do, they do not participate in the process.

WHAT STUDENT SURVEY DATA SAY ABOUT ACADEMIC ADVISING

Whether one conceives of the O'Banion model of academic advising as linear or integrated, there is little disagreement among practitioners that the five steps— (1 and 2) exploration of life and vocational goals, (3) program choice, (4) course choice, and (5) scheduling—are the hallmarks of a well-designed academic advising system. Student self-reported data, both at the aggregate level and disaggregated by race, ethnicity, gender, enrollment status, developmental status, and other variables, can provide powerful insights for colleges committed to improving their students' academic advising experiences—and to promoting college completion.

Exploration of Life and Vocational Goals

Entering students are not systematically engaging in the processes of examining life and vocational goals. Half (50%) of entering students reported that they are aware of career counseling, and among those who are aware, 82% said they have not used career counseling by the end of their first 3 weeks in college. In concrete terms, for every 100 entering students, just 50 were aware of career counseling, and only 9 students met with a career counselor by the end of their first 3 weeks (CCCSE, 2012c). In addition to the core SENSE survey, colleges may administer optional special-focus modules. Two of these modules—Academic Advising and Planning and Student Success Courses—render additional relevant data.

Data from the SENSE special-focus module on Academic Advising and Planning provide deeper insight into how little entering students are experiencing systematic life and vocational planning. Even though the data from more experienced students are somewhat more positive than those from entering students, findings suggest that substantial improvement or redesign is indicated. When asked to indicate how much their colleges helped them gain information about career opportunities, 23% of CCSSE respondents said their colleges helped them "very much," 38% responded "quite a bit," and 29% reported "some." However, 19% reported that their colleges helped them "very little" to gain information about career opportunities (CCCSE, 2011). Across the board, students reported that they are unlikely to participate in academic advising that consistently incorporates exploration of life and vocational goals.

Program Choice, Course Choice, and Scheduling

SENSE data reveal that, for most entering students, the academic advising process they engage with is one that falls substantially short of that proposed by the O'Banion model. Not only do few students have the opportunity to explore life and vocational goals, but they overwhelmingly reported that their interactions with advisors (when they meet with an advisor) are more likely to consist of selecting courses than exploring programs of study. As O'Banion noted, the Center's data substantiate that most students' academic advising experience begins at step three: program choice. Table 2.3 summarizes responses of entering students to SENSE and the Academic Advising and Planning module. Students' responses tell

Table 2.3 ◆ Entering Students' Responses to SENSE Items on the Academic Advising Experience

Survey Item	Response	
	Agree/ Strongly Agree	Disagree/ Strongly Disagree
SENSE Academic Planning and Advising Module		
A college staff member spent enough time with me to help me understand the process of enrolling and attending college.	51%	25%
A college staff member talked with me about the importance of completing a certificate or degree.	49%	36%
A college staff member explained core courses and other requirements for completing a certificate/degree, or transferring to another college/university.	49%	28%
A college staff member helped me to design a course sequence that showed how long it would take to attain my educational goals.	38%	37%
A college staff member helped me to understand how much money I am likely to earn through a job in my selected major/career field.	32%	53%
A college staff member helped me to understand where [geographic location] I am likely to find employment in my selected major/career field.	19%	57%
A staff member explained how placement test scores are used to determine if I was ready for college-level courses or needed to take courses to help me become college ready.	61%	18%
A college staff member clearly explained to me where to find help if I were considering dropping out of or withdrawing from college.	44%	37%
A college staff member clearly explained consequences of receiving poor grades (academic probation, potential loss of financial assistance or scholarships, etc.).	55%	25%
A college staff member helped me understand approximately how many hours outside of class (per week) I need to spend preparing and studying for each course I am taking.	48%	30%
SENSE		
An advisor helped me identify the courses I needed to take during my first term.	70%	—
A staff member talked with me about my outside commitments to determine how many courses to take.	26%	48%
An advisor helped me select a course of study, program, or major.	59%	—
An advisor helped me set academic goals and create a plan for achieving them.	38%	—

Note. Adapted from CCCSE (2012b, 2012c).

us that, for the most part, the complex and critically important process of academic advising has been reduced to an interaction with a college staff person—counselor, advisor, or other—primarily characterized by selecting courses without consideration for students' varied, and often substantial, outside commitments and also without thoughtful consideration of goal setting and the path to goal achievement.

RETHINKING ACADEMIC ADVISING: A JUST-IN-TIME APPROACH

As the data suggest, academic advising in many colleges is a one-time event (if, indeed, a student even meets with an advisor) consisting mainly of selecting courses and, to a lesser extent, selecting a major or course of study. Effective academic advising, by contrast, is a process consisting of periodic interactions between the student and trained counselors, advisors, faculty, other college staff, or students—or combinations of such people, each with particular advising roles. What can colleges do differently to improve their systems of academic advising? How can they adequately engage students in academic advising, given students' substantial outside commitments?

One thing colleges can and should do is to break academic advising down into manageable pieces whereby students are given necessary information not all at once, but as they need it—a just-in-time system. Ideally, the process should begin weeks before the start of classes, and SENSE data indicate that colleges have an excellent opportunity to make this happen. O'Banion suggests that colleges use a team-based approach and preenrollment sessions for groups of students so that students can engage in the necessary work of beginning to analyze their life and vocational goals.

The majority of entering students (86%) reported that they registered for classes during their first term more than 1 week before classes began (CCCSE, 2012c). What are colleges doing with students who have already completed the registration process? How are they engaging with them—or not? If students have not, as the data depict, spent time exploring life, academic, and vocational goals, how can colleges turn this "down time" into something that helps students build a stronger foundation for academic success? How might a well-designed *mandatory* orientation experience, with a just-in-time focus on academic advising and planning, help more students to at least begin developing the skills and roadmaps necessary for success? How can a college redesign the one experience—orientation—that all students can be required to take part in to initiate the important work of exploring life and vocational goals?

The data regarding orientation once again paint a picture of missed opportunity and need for redesign of policies and practice. While 96% of colleges reported having implemented orientation, just 38% indicated that attendance is required for all first-time (full- and part-time) students (CCCSE, 2012a). Because orientation is typically an optional activity, many students simply opt out of participation. Data bear this out: More than half of entering students (55%) reported that they did not attend an on-campus orientation prior to the start of classes, and nearly one quarter (24%) indicated that they were unable to participate in orientation because of scheduling or other issues. Perhaps most disheartening is this: 18% of entering students said they were unaware of their college's orientation (CCCSE, 2012c). Not surprisingly, there is both statistical and practical significance in students' responses to these items when the data are disaggregated by enrollment status: 51% of full-time and 41% of part-time students attended an orientation on campus before their first class; 14% of full-time versus 21% of part-time students were unaware of an orientation.

Examining these data by enrollment status illustrates the differences in entering students' experiences based on whether they attend college full or part time. While full-time students are more likely to be engaged with their college's orientation programs than are their part-time peers, the reality is that community colleges typically enroll more part-time than full-time students. A comprehensive—and mandatory—orientation program can be an ideal venue for forging important early relationships with students (and helping them to connect with other students, faculty, and staff) and for engaging students in the critical work of examining their life, academic, and vocational goals. Institutional policies requiring students to register earlier, thereby creating a longer time period for colleges to initiate the academic advising and planning process, are both indicated and possible. Imagine if every community college had 2–3 weeks prior to the beginning of class to orient students effectively—to get them starting right! Other colleges and universities have traditionally required students to spend a week on campus in orientation and advising before classes begin. Why would community college students not need some form of required orientation and advising?

Colleges also can establish systems for keeping students engaged with academic advising, thus enabling students to continue building and mastering the skills and competencies initiated during their earlier interactions. One of the primary means by which colleges can do this is to take services traditionally offered through the student affairs office and move them into the classroom. By bringing services to the students and building experiences into the classroom, colleges can continue to strengthen student engagement not only with academic advising and planning, but also with other students, faculty, staff, and the students' course work—all of which are critical components of success.

No matter what the course or experience is called, and this varies quite substantially, a well-designed and implemented student success course, learning community, or first-year experience can be the ideal setting for keeping the important work of academic advising going once courses begin. While just 27% of entering students reported enrolling in a course specifically designed to teach skills and strategies to help them succeed in college (e.g., a college success or student success course), available data indicate that students find these courses helpful in a number of important ways (CCCSE, 2012c). In every case, entering students who reported enrolling in a college success course are much more likely, in both practical and statistical terms, to experience crucial aspects of the academic planning and advising process, as is shown in Table 2.4.

Data mined from entering students responding to the SENSE Student Success Courses special-focus module provide additional information about how student success courses can be used to extend the academic planning and advising process post enrollment. Selected highlights from entering student respondents who indicated that they enrolled in a student success course (e.g., student success, student development, freshman seminar, extended orientation, study skills, or student life skills) during their first academic term are presented in Table 2.5.

These data demonstrate the potential of a well-designed and thoughtfully implemented student success course for improving academic advising and student success, as they reflect a far richer academic advising experience than the one typically reported by entering students. Yet data from colleges indicate that, despite the usefulness of these courses or programs, they are not widely integrated into the typical student experience. Eighty-three percent of colleges responding

Table 2.4 ◆ Comparison of the Advising Experience for Entering Students With or Without a Success Course

Survey Item	Success Course Taken	
	yes	no
Never used academic advising.	27%	32%
Never used career counseling.	69%	63%
An advisor helped student select a course of study, program, or major.	63%	58%
An advisor helped student set academic goals and create a plan for achieving them.	42%	37%
An advisor helped student to identify the courses to take during first term.	74%	68%
A staff member talked with student about outside commitments to help student figure out the number of courses to take.	31%	24%

Note. Adapted from CCCSE (2012c).

Table 2.5 ◆ Entering Students' Responses to SENSE Module Items on Student Success Courses

Survey Item	Agree/ Strongly Agree
Course helped me understand my academic strengths and weaknesses.	62%
Course helped me develop a written academic plan for achieving my academic goals.	54%
Course helped me develop skills to become a better student.	70%
Course helped me feel more connected to the college.	64%
Course helped me learn about important college policies and deadlines.	69%
Course helped me learn about college services available to help students succeed.	71%
Course should be mandatory for all new students.	54%

Note. Adapted from CCCSE (2012d).

to the Community College Institutional Survey reported that they offer a student success course, but just 15% (35 of 238 colleges) reported that the course is mandatory for all first-time, full- and part-time, students (CCCSE, 2012a). Taken together, these results reinforce the necessity of system redesign. Simply adding a student success course to an institution's offerings will not be effective. Rather, these data help to bring to light the need for rethinking the overall design of how, when, where, and through whom colleges engage students in the process of academic advising and planning.

RECOMMENDATIONS FOR EFFECTIVE ADVISING

Despite colleges' efforts, the overwhelming majority of entering community college students pass through their college's doors unaware of expectations, unaffected by the services colleges think they provide, and unaided in making decisions that will significantly determine their success as students. Relying on family and friends (who may be armed with incorrect information), they select majors or programs of study without thoroughly understanding the consequences of their choices, or they simply wander through the curriculum. Uninformed about important matters such as the ability to earn a living wage in their selected field— or the likelihood of transferring credits to a 4-year institution—they forge ahead. Enthusiastically believing that they have both the motivation and academic preparation to succeed, entering students register for often-unrealistic course loads without due consideration for their outside-of-college commitments.

The data presented in this chapter represent only a sample of the findings drawn from surveys and students focus groups conducted by the Center. Overall, results suggest a handful of steps colleges should consider as they rethink and redesign advising processes.

1. Design from the student's point of view. What advising is needed, at what point in time, available from whom and through what medium?
2. Unpack advising into its crucial component parts. Design each of the critical advising functions as a continuing chronological process. Advising is indeed a process, not an event.

3. Apply ingenuity in designing group advising approaches. The reality is that fiscal constraints will not accommodate hiring large numbers of new advisors to implement a traditional one-on-one advising model. The good news is that group advising can be good for students when colleges figure out how to optimize student-to-student engagement as well as advisor-student engagement in advising groups.

4. Analyze the components of the advising system to match delivery mode (Online? Face to face? Both?) with content and to deploy human resources (professional advisors, faculty advisors, student peer advisors) most effectively.

5. Understand that students do not know what they do not know. Use data to help students understand why the institution mandates certain experiences. Students enroll with the expectation of doing well. And they trust that college staff and faculty are the experts, giving them the best possible advice.

6. Act on the axiom that "students don't do optional" (McClenney & Arnsparger, 2012, p. 57). Continuing to rely on the traditional referral model will not work. Integrating a comprehensive, continuing, and inescapable advising experience into "what it means to go to college here" is essential.

The academic advising function in its most comprehensive and effective form can no longer be characterized as a transaction whereby a college staff member—or a computer screen—merely assists students in registering for courses. Colleges must begin to find ways to engage entering students in a holistic approach of planning for their academic and vocational futures if we are ever to make needed improvement in course, certificate, and program completion.

REFERENCES

ACT. (2010). *What works in student retention? Fourth national survey. Community colleges report.* Retrieved from http://www.act.org/research/policymakers/pdf/droptables/commmunitycolleges.pdf

American Association of Community Colleges. (2013). *Community college fact sheet.* Available from http://www.aacc.nche.edu/aboutcc/pages/fastfacts.aspx

Astin, A. W. (1984). Student involvement: A developmental theory for higher education. *Journal of College Student Personnel, 25*, 298–307.

Center for Community College Student Engagement. (2011). 2011 community college survey of engagement (CCSSE) cohort results [Data file]. Retrieved from http://www.ccsse.org/members/reports/2011/reports.cfm

Center for Community College Student Engagement. (2012a). 2011 and 2012 community college institutional survey results [Data file]. Retrieved from http://www.ccsse.org/members/reports/2011/reports.cfm

Center for Community College Student Engagement. (2012b). 2011 survey of entering student engagement (SENSE) academic planning and advising special-focus module results [Data file]. Retrieved from http://www.ccsse.org/sense/members/reports/2011/reports.cfm

Center for Community College Student Engagement. (2012c). 2011 survey of entering student engagement (SENSE) cohort results [Data file]. Retrieved from http://www.ccsse.org/sense/members/reports/2011/reports.cfm

Center for Community College Student Engagement. (2012d). 2011 survey of entering student engagement (SENSE) student success courses special-focus module results [Data file]. Retrieved from http://www.ccsse.org/sense/members/reports/2011/reports.cfm

Clery, S., & Topper, A. (2008, September/October). Students earning zero credits. *Data Notes, 3*(5). Retrieved from http://www.achievingthedream.org/dataresearch/datanotesnewsletter/default.tp

Frost, S. H. (1991). *Academic advising for student success: A system of shared responsibility* (ASHE-ERIC Higher Education Report No. 3). Washington, DC: George Washington University, School of Education and Human Development. (ERIC # ED340274)

McClenney, K. M., & Arnsparger, A. (2012). *Students speak: Are we listening?* Austin, TX: Center for Community College Student Engagement.

McClenney, K. M., & Marti, C. M. (2006). *Exploring relationships between student engagement and student outcomes in community colleges: Report on validation research* [Working paper]. Austin, TX: Center for Community College Student Engagement. Retrieved from http://www.ccsse.org/publications/CCSSE%20Working%20Paper%20on%20Validation%20Research%20December%202006.pdf

McCormick, A., & McClenney, K. (2012, Winter). Will these trees ever bear fruit? A response to the special issue on student engagement. *The Review of Higher Education, 35*(2), 307–333.

Pascarella, E. T. (1980). Student-faculty informal contact and college outcomes. *Review of Educational Research, 50,* 545–595.

Pascarella, E. T. (1985). College environmental influences on learning and cognitive development. In J. C. Smart (Ed.), *Higher education: Handbook of theory and research* (vol. 2, pp. 1–61). New York: Agathon Press.

Terenzini, P. T., Pascarella, E. T., & Lorang, W. G. (1982). An assessment of the academic and social influences on freshman year educational outcomes. *The Review of Higher Education, 5,* 86–109.

Tinto, V. (1987). *Leaving college: Rethinking the causes and cures of student attrition.* Chicago: University of Chicago Press.

CHAPTER 3

Valencia College:
A Learning-
Centered Student
Advising System

Joyce C. Romano

Valencia College, located in Orange and Osceola Counties in Central Florida, is a public, comprehensive community college that provides opportunities for academic, technical, and lifelong learning in a collaborative culture dedicated to inquiry, results, and excellence. In 2010–2011, approximately 71,000 students took courses at seven campus or center locations. Valencia provides associate degree programs that prepare learners to succeed in university studies; courses and services that provide learners with the right start in their college careers; and associate degree, certificate, bachelor's, and continuing professional education programs that prepare learners for entering and progressing in the workforce.

L IFEMAP IS A DEVELOPMENTAL ADVISING model and system that promotes student social and academic integration, education and career planning, and acquisition of study and life skills. LifeMap integrates all college faculty, staff, and resources into a unified system to create a normative expectation and focus of students' efforts to develop life, career, and education plans early in their college experience. LifeMap was developed at Valencia College in the mid-1990s as the college began to explore a new approach to developmental advising that was part of a Title III grant. Starting in 1995, Valencia also launched a learning-centered journey by holding broad discussions throughout the college on what it meant to be a learning-centered college (see Kilingman, Castellano, & Kelley, 2008). Valencia connected with other colleges that were exploring this concept through the 1995 "Leadership and Institutional Transformation" initiative funded by the American Council on Education and the Kellogg Foundation and continued the momentum when Valencia was selected as one of 12 of the League for Innovation's Vanguard Learning Colleges in 2000. Through this work, Valencia reviewed and revised many college systems with a focus on the two questions: "How does this action improve and expand student learning? How do we know this action improves and expands student learning?" (O'Banion, 1997).

LifeMap was one of the new systems that emerged from this learning-centered journey. Valencia was motivated by its dissatisfaction with results in the completion of developmental education and graduation rates, particularly among students from disadvantaged backgrounds who are a critical part of the community. The college was also concerned about the fragmentation of student services among the multiple campuses.

Early exploration of developmental advising was informed by *Academic Advising for Student Success: A System of Shared Responsibility* (Frost, 1991), which was discussed by multiple teams of faculty and staff in reading circles. The teams were Intrigued by the author's ideas that faculty's understanding of students' goals was critical to students' motivation in class, to think of "advising as teaching," and the importance of "advising alliances" to support student success. Valencia drew on these ideas to develop a Title III grant proposal to strengthen the institution by further exploring the application of these ideas at the college. Susan Frost, author of the book and then director of institutional planning and research at Emory University, served as a consultant to the 5-year Title III grant (1994–1999) and encouraged Valencia to fundamentally change the student experience rather than "tinkering on the edges." The design of the Title III work included teams of faculty and staff who studied together and designed interventions applicable to their professional practice (curricular or co-curricular) that they implemented with students and then assessed the results.

Motivated by Frost's advice, the teams studied the research of leading higher education professionals and brought many of them to campus to discuss their findings and ideas. They then reflected on how they related to our professional practice and developed pilot projects to test our ideas. Although informed by all of the higher education professionals studied, LifeMap is clearly influenced by research on college choice (Hossler & Schmidt, 1990), academic and social integration as a correlate of student persistence (Tinto, 1993), academic advising models (O'Banion, 1994), and career development models (Gordon & Sears, 1997), as well as Frost's ideas on advising as teaching and the importance of advising alliances. Near the end of the 5-year cycle, Valencia had developed a coherent system that would change the way in which it engaged students and present to students in their earliest interactions with the college its expectations for their learning and progression.

In 1999, the marketing department branded LifeMap with the tag line, "Life's a trip. You'll need directions." Since that time, Valencia has developed a comprehensive system that aligns all of its programs, procedures, services, and people to the stages of LifeMap and the cultural expectation that students will develop life, career, and education goals and plans early in their college experience. The system includes branding and marketing campaigns, printed materials, program development, online planning tools, procedural alignment, and, most importantly, faculty and staff development that prepares all of Valencia to support students' engagement with LifeMap. The comprehensive nature of the system means that it is in a continuous state of assessment, development, and improvement. LifeMap will never be "finished," because students and staff are continually changing and evolving.

THE LIFEMAP MODEL

Developmental advising is the term Valencia uses to describe the process that students are in as they enter, progress, and move beyond Valencia to their next educational or vocational destination. *Developmental* is meant in the sense of human development, rather than the way the term is used to refer to those students who start in courses below college level, as is signified by the term *developmental education*. The definition is described in the LifeMap mission statement as follows:

> *A system of shared responsibilities between students and the college that results in social and academic integration, education and career plans, and the acquisition of study and life skills.*

Beginning in 1999, LifeMap implementation and development has included mapping programs and services to the LifeMap model; developing new programs identified through gap analysis based on the LifeMap stages; intensive and ongoing faculty and staff development; a consistent and creative marketing of LifeMap to current students; and the development of Atlas, Valencia's student portal. Atlas is the digital expression of LifeMap that supports LifeMap's goal of student self-sufficiency by providing students access to their education information; My LifeMap tools for developing and saving career and education plans; online connection with faculty, staff, and other students; and direction to complete their career and education plans.

LifeMap recognizes that students typically enter college with vague notions of their goals and minimal understanding of how to negotiate the college environment. With the goal of self-sufficiency, LifeMap provides more support for students in the beginning of their college experience with the explicit expectation that they take responsibility for their education and move toward becoming more self-directed in a developmental sequence. To visually explain this expectation to students and staff, we use the "Big *A* to the Big *S*" diagram *(A As AS aS S)*, which is included in the LifeMap student handbook and described at new student orientation. It is made clear to students that, although it is normal for them to look for experts in the environment when they first arrive *(A* = advisor), they are expected to "own" their education journey and join the advising alliance *(As =*

advisor + student) as they register and begin classes. They are expected to work toward increased self-sufficiency using online and other tools that they can review with an advisor *(AS)*, gaining in personal competence *(aS)* until they become fully self-directed *(S)* and able to negotiate the next education or work system that they enter based on what they have learned at Valencia.

Advisor is used generically in this context to mean anyone at Valencia whom a student may approach for assistance. This could be a custodian, security officer, faculty member, academic advisor, or library assistant. Academic advising is formally provided through the Student Affairs office by professional academic advisors, career advisors, student services advisors, career program advisors, and counselors. While most advising is provided face to face, online advising is available, including through a chat feature. Counselors are faculty and earn continuing contracts through the same teaching and learning academy and tenure process as faculty and librarians. Besides providing one-to-one advising, counselors design curriculum and learning assessments, lead programs, provide workshops, support special student populations, and consult with faculty on student issues.

Both advisors and counselors report to the deans of students on each campus. The deans of students have primary responsibility for the advising program. Because the ratio of advisors to students is 520 to 1, at Valencia, teaching faculty members are key partners in LifeMap because they have close interactions with 150–200 students in their classes each semester. Although they do not have any formal responsibility for advising students, faculty can convey the cultural expectation that students develop career and education plans and use the college resources to support that planning.

STAGES AND SUCCESS INDICATORS

LifeMap describes for students what they should do when for each of five stages. Each stage includes an outcome, performance indicators, and guiding principles tied to the literature and research on best practices. (Details of the LifeMap stages may be viewed on the Valencia College website.) The stages and success indicators are summarized in the following sections.

Stage 1. College Transition

Students are learning about college choice and requirements, usually starting in middle school or early high school, and develop a personal sense that college is possible as well as learn the details of what they need to do academically, financially, and procedurally to make a smooth transition into college and the first day of class.

Success Indicators

♦ Explain why a college education is possible for you.

♦ Fully engage in the enrollment process: timely completion of application, assessment, orientation, financial aid, and registration for classes prior to priority deadlines.

♦ Make initial choices about education and career interests.

♦ Discuss education and career interests with advisors and others.

♦ Establish a financial plan for obtaining a college education.

♦ Complete assessment for appropriate placement in reading, mathematics, and English.

Stage 2. Introduction to College

Students enrolled in their first 15 credit hours of college course work are making important transitions and connections that will impact success at Valencia. Valencia assists students in the beginning of their college careers to make the connections and follow the directions needed to plan a successful college experience.

Success Indicators

♦ Develop, save, and follow an education plan that will guide course selection toward degree completion using My Education Plan (described later in the chapter).

♦ Successfully complete (with an *A, B,* or *C*) all course work in which enrolled.

- Reduce the number of remaining preparatory courses each term by enrolling in the next level of the sequence until completion.

- Create and follow a study plan for each enrolled course.

- Use campus resources (writing centers, tutoring, library, Skillshops, etc.).

- Identify life goals by completing the LifeMap student handbook exercise.

- Identify and research a potential career path using My Career Planner.

- Engage with students, staff, advisors, and faculty on campus.

- Participate in campus activities or organizations.

- Write down intended graduation date.

Stage 3. Progression to Degree

Students enrolled while completing 16–44 credit hours of college course work are implementing career and education plans and confirming decisions about their goals. Students benefit from exploring, adjusting, or confirming their career and education goals and connecting with Valencia resources to enhance their education experience.

Success Indicators

- Revise education plan as needed, documenting progression toward goal.

- Determine career options in My Career Planner.

- Develop financial literacy and a financial plan for continued education and life after graduation using My Financial Planner.

- Complete general education requirements.

- Examine and reflect on what you learned in terms of the defined program learning outcomes for chosen degree.

- If seeking an associate of arts degree to transfer to an upper-division program, determine prerequisites that may be needed for intended degree at the transfer institution.

- Explore chosen career field by participating in internships, job shadowing, information interviews, volunteer experiences, or by conducting Internet searches.

- Explore options for continued education or employment after graduation.

- Maintain social connections on campus with staff, students, advisors, and faculty.

- Continue to participate in campus activities or organizations.

Stage 4. Graduation Transition

Students enrolled while completing 45 credit hours and beyond are completing their degrees and making plans for transfer to complete a bachelor's degree or preparing to enter the workforce. Students preparing for this transition can connect with Valencia resources to assist in this process.

Success Indicators

- Confirm the term you are graduating.

- Complete an associate degree without exceeding the required number of credit hours by more than 15%.

- Apply for graduation by the appropriate deadline.

- Create a portfolio using My Portfolio that demonstrates achievements and skills.

- Document achievement of Valencia's core competencies in My Portfolio.

- Prepare a plan for continuing education or employment after graduation from Valencia.

- Complete the first step in career plan.

- Write a résumé that documents educational and workplace achievements and skills.

- Review résumé with career advisor or counselor.

- Update My Portfolio and create a "public view" that demonstrates your achievement and skills.

- Gather recommendation letters from staff, advisors, and faculty.

- Communicate to others what you have learned and what you can do orally and in writing.

- Maintain social connections made at Valencia with staff, students, advisors, and faculty for references and future opportunities.

- Document changes (technological, practices, laws, budgets, etc.) that may occur between the associate degree and employment.

Stage 5. Lifelong Learning

After students transition into the workforce, they will discover the need for continued learning, retooling of skills and knowledge, and the need to create new skills. Students will be able to recreate the cycle of setting goals, evaluating options, identifying additional education needs, and acting to meet those education needs at Valencia or other education institutions.

Success Indicators

- Set goals that reflect ability to think critically, evaluate opportunities, identify additional education needs, and act to meet those education needs at Valencia.

- Document professional development by maintaining a résumé and portfolio that reflect continual improvement.

- In periods of career transition, retooling, or acquiring new skills, reengage the cycle of goal setting, career development, and education planning learned at Valencia.

- Build and maintain professional networks.

While most of the LifeMap model development occurred through grant-funded activities, Valencia was motivated to keep the momentum going by fully implementing the LifeMap model into an integrated system that would transform the

Valencia student experience. Three systems were integrated in the model. The first system, LifeMap, can be described through the elements of programs and services, marketing, publications, professional development, and funding. Atlas, the online learning support portal, was the second major system that Valencia designed and implemented to support LifeMap. The third major system design focused on the way in which Valencia engages students through learning-centered student services. These systems are described in more detail in the following sections.

THE LIFEMAP SYSTEM

Programs and Services

Valencia programs and services are mapped to each of the stages to support the success indicators (student learning outcomes). A review of the programs and services will show that some departments, such as the career center, will be listed in several of the stages, although the specific programs and services within that department are tailored to the appropriate LifeMap stage. Other programs are specific to a particular stage, such as the RoadMap to Success Award that was designed for first-year students. This award program includes a specific developmental advising curriculum in which a student works with an academic advisor or counselor, attends co-curricular programs, and successfully completes his or her course work in order to earn a $500 award. The process of mapping programs and services to the LifeMap model helped Valencia identify gaps in programs and services in order to support students in achieving the learning outcomes of each stage.

By design, there are more intentional interventions in "Introduction to College," as this is a time when students are becoming acclimated to their college experience and we expect their relationship to be more dependent on college experts for assistance *(As)*. As another example of the alignment work, Valencia added communications and prompts to "Graduation Transition" to encourage students to successfully complete their degree and prepare for the next steps in their career and education paths *(aS)*.

Skillshops is another program that reflects the LifeMap brand (see Valencia, 2013c). Co-curricular workshops are offered each term in categories of academic enhancement, education planning, Valencia resources, tutorials and training, career development, cultural and social awareness, and personal development. For example, there were 295 workshops offered in spring 2012. Students can attend on their own; may attend to earn credit toward class or scholarship requirements; or may be referred to the workshops by faculty, advisors, or counselors. Faculty can arrange for the workshop presenters to validate student attendance. Skillshops creates an organizing infrastructure and promotional venue for many areas of the college that wish to engage students in informational or developmental programs.

LifeMap is the organizing system for all programs and services including student development, career centers, students with disabilities, international students, internships, and workforce services. The LifeMap brand is included when developing print and online materials so that it presents to students the unified system of programs and services that support the central theme of career and education planning.

Publications

LifeMap links written publications designed to assist students in achieving their career and education goals. The LifeMap student handbook was first produced in 1999 to explain LifeMap to students and integrate resource information that was developed by faculty and advisors as part of the original grant work. Since then, a new staff group annually reviews and revises the content based on student, faculty, and staff feedback and publishes the LifeMap student handbook, which is printed and distributed to students and posted online. The LifeMap student handbook (Valencia, 2013a) is specifically designed based on one of the theories Valencia adopted in developing the LifeMap model. O'Banion (1994) proposed an ideal model of academic advising in which students begin with determining their life goals, defining compatible career goals followed by education goals, and then developing a class schedule. While this is not the normal order in which most students approach the advising system, Valencia models this ideal progression through the LifeMap student handbook as it describes the planning process in this order and provides self-assessments so that students can respond to, reflect on, and document their learning. The handbook also provides a weekly appointment calendar with key academic dates along with prompts to remind students of tasks to complete each week that are aligned with each of the LifeMap stages.

In 2002, Valencia followed the advice of an outside consultant who was impressed with the student handbook and wondered why the college did not have a corollary publication for faculty. The LifeMap faculty guidebook is now published annually and provides a weekly appointment calendar for faculty embedded with just-in-time LifeMap information to share with their students as well as key academic dates. The guidebook also includes sections on important dates and deadlines; classroom connection information such as learning assessments, Web resources and tools, and examples of integrated LifeMap learning opportunities that faculty have implemented in specific courses; and faculty resources such as faculty development, college initiative descriptions, a campus directory, and the college strategic plan.

Marketing

From the early introduction of LifeMap, Valencia has considered the process to be one of "cultural adoption" in which a variety of elements must be addressed in order to make LifeMap a part of the everyday life of Valencia students. LifeMap is deliberately marketed to students to encourage their exploration and use of the system to support their planning process. As with any other brand, marketing must be renewed and refreshed periodically. The current campaign was designed and implemented by Valencia's marketing department in January 2010 and will be renewed in 2013. The basis of the current campaign is that LifeMap is a process that each student should design for him- or herself. This evolved from earlier campaigns in which students tended to look for LifeMap as a thing ("Where do I go to get my LifeMap?"). The latest campaign focused on how to introduce students to examples of ways in which they could interact with LifeMap to develop a plan unique to themselves and their interests.

Six student guides represent unique life paths and challenges through large, colorful murals on college windows and hallways that depict a point of view that each student is experiencing. For example, "Jordan" knows he wants to be a doctor but does not know all that he needs to get to that goal. One of his murals says, "Becoming a doctor is the big picture. I've just got to work out the details like how to pay for all that school." Another example is "Erica," a single mom who is juggling a lot of responsibility. One of her murals says, "Teaching will take a lot of focus and discipline. Luckily between two kids, working, and school, I'll have plenty of practice." "Eddie" likes all of the social aspects of college and struggles to focus on the academic work. One of his murals on the advising center's waiting area wall says, "I'd rather spend time sitting here than sitting in the wrong classes later."

All of the murals direct students to the Atlas tool, Me in the Making, which presents a musical flash video introducing LifeMap and then links to the Atlas sign-on page where students can get to the Me in Making site. The site provides a searchable function for all of Atlas, provides links that show how each of the six student guides is using LifeMap (as examples that students can follow), and provides links to Valencia's and other websites organized by popular links, college survival, money matters, education planning, career planning, and making connections. The next LifeMap campaign will continue to build on student use of the system and how to present the brand to encourage wider and deeper cultural adoption.

Professional Development

Faculty and staff development is another major component of the LifeMap system. Understanding LifeMap purpose, stages, theory, and elements is a fundamental part of the professional training for all student affairs staff at Valencia. Student Affairs implements an annual professional development program that includes three professional development days in which all student affairs staff gather to learn updates and strengthen skills. In addition, every Friday morning an hour is set aside for professional development for all student affairs staff in which managers hold group meetings or assign individual development programs. LifeMap is one of six named competencies for all student affairs staff and is included in annual professional development plans and evaluation. Staff attend workshops on and off campus that support their individual professional development plans.

LifeMap is also one of seven core competencies for all new faculty at Valencia. Faculty who are hired under continuing contract participate in a 3-year induction process that includes learning about the seven competencies and creating a portfolio that documents their understanding and professional practice related to each competency, including LifeMap. Beyond demonstrating competency in LifeMap (which all continuing contract faculty must complete), Student Affairs sponsors an annual recognition award for the LifeMap Exemplary Faculty Portfolio. As part of the overall faculty development program, there are a series of courses on LifeMap and a narrated online presentation that any faculty member can view to learn about LifeMap (see Valencia, 2013b). Student Affairs has also sponsored stipend-supported annual seminars for full-time and adjunct faculty who want to learn more about LifeMap and who agree to design and implement an integrated LifeMap activity in their class. A LifeMap certificate is under development for faculty and staff, which will require completion of several LifeMap courses including integration into professional practice and will be an option in Valencia's faculty and staff development program.

Funding

Funding for LifeMap is integrated into operational budgets in student affairs, marketing, faculty development, and information technology. Student activity funds provide an important source of funding for programs such as RoadMap to Success awards (scholarship program), the LifeMap student handbook and LifeMap faculty guidebook, Skillshops and new student orientation materials, the peer leaders who staff the welcome teams, information stations, Atlas access labs and peer educators, and the LifeMap marketing campaigns. Because LifeMap is a central initiative of Valencia, resources are regularly devoted to sustaining and continually updating the system.

THE ATLAS PORTAL

Atlas (Valencia's online learning portal) was the second system designed to support LifeMap using the design of "connection and direction." Atlas tabs are organized to connect students to the information, people, and resources they need to develop and implement their career and education plans. Atlas provides connection for students, faculty, and advising staff through Atlas e-mail, course chat and discussion groups, and Atlas groups. Atlas e-mails are used as the primary and official mode of communication between students and professionals at Valencia. Following a carefully designed schedule, Atlas sends information, reminders, and just-in-time prompts to guide students through enrollment and progression processes. For example, an e-mail is sent when grades are posted each term that also encourages students to check their degree audits and update their education plan at that time. The content on Atlas is continually reviewed and revised by a staff group based on feedback from students, faculty, and advisors as to what is useful and what is not clear to students. Atlas, like LifeMap, is a continuous work in progress.

Atlas provides direction through the My LifeMap tools that were custom designed at Valencia. My Career Planner allows students to conduct self-assessments on values, skills, and interests; match those assessments to career options; and save the results of exploration so that it can be discussed with a career counselor and referred to at a later time. My Education Plan allows students to develop a specific degree course plan based on a transfer plan for associate in arts degrees or associate in science programs and then map that degree plan over time so that courses are organized in sequence for each semester of enrollment. After creating their education plan, students can click a button to e-mail the plan to an advisor who will review it online and provide feedback to the student. My Financial Plan provides a tutorial on financial literacy so that students can develop a financial plan for their education. My Job Prospects provides a search engine based on career interests and projected job outlook by geographical area so students can plan for their future employment. My Portfolio provides a template for students to document examples of their accomplishments, create a résumé, and share their online portfolio with potential employers or others. All Valencia students can use the My LifeMap tools through their Atlas accounts. My LifeMap tools are integrated into the curriculum and co-curriculum in a variety of ways, including class assignments, required for process approval (such as financial aid standards of academic progress appeals), or reviewed when meeting with an advisor or counselor.

LEARNING-CENTERED STUDENT SERVICES

The third system redesign, after LifeMap and Atlas, focused on the delivery of student services and was implemented in 2003 in order to engage students in learning each overall process within LifeMap (e.g., enrollment, graduation) instead of responding to isolated questions (e.g., "Where can I get a transcript?"). Valencia arrived at this model after studying the business literature on process reengineering and system redesign (Hammer & Champy, 1993; Hammer & Stanton, 1995).

Students who come to campus for student services start in the Answer Center and engage in integrated student services provided by cross-trained advisors (admissions, advising, and financial aid). Students who need more in-depth assistance go to student services to meet with specialists such as academic advisors, counselors, financial aid specialists, international advisors, or veterans advisors who are located in the same office suite. District offices in admissions and financial aid include staff with expertise in back office processing who can work without constant interruption. Students' phone calls are answered by a call center of cross-trained staff in a central location. Career centers, assessment, and students with disabilities are still specialized service areas. Student peers provide general direction in the information station (centrally located information desk) and Atlas access labs (assistance with using the Atlas system). In 2010–2011, 16,000 new students attended the mandatory new student orientation. In that year, there were 207,700 student visits to the Answer Center, 81,500 academic advising in-person contacts, and 237,128 calls to the call centers.

The major design goal of this delivery system is to provide one physical location where students can learn the overall process and understand their next steps facilitated by a student services advisor who knows the entire process and not just one piece of it. Atlas is an important component in this system, and there are always people to assist as needed. This is another example of helping students move toward self-sufficiency *(AS)*. Another goal of the redesign was to designate staffers whose main responsibility is back-office processing rather than direct meetings with students, and to separate levels of service by the depth of help students need rather than by administrative units. In the original design, Valencia thought it was separating the quick questions and answers from the more in-depth discussions, but anyone who has worked in student services knows that there really are no quick questions and answers due to the complexity of higher education systems and regulations.

Physical space on the campuses was redesigned to fit the new model with an improvement in personal connection (individual kiosks rather than long counters in the answer centers); closer working relationships (counselors and financial aid specialists in the same office space as student services); and the visible information stations in each lobby through which peer leaders provide directions, written materials, forms, and a friendly face.

LIFEMAP EVALUATION

The evaluation of LifeMap and its impact on student learning and success is another major and ongoing component. As part of its learning-centered initiative, which has been ongoing since Valencia began its discussion of developmental advising, LifeMap has certainly contributed to gains in traditional institutional effectiveness measures:

- Fall-to-spring persistence of new students increased from 79% in 2002 to 86% in 2010.

- Fall-to-fall persistence of new students increased from 58% in 2002 to 65% in 2009.

- New student completion of 30 college credits in 3 years increased from 43% in 1997 to 57% in 2008.

- New student associate degree graduation rates in 5 years increased from 23% in 1997 to 33% in 2008.

- From 2002 to 2010, developmental education sequence completion in 2 years increased from 4% in reading to 80%; 7% in writing to 78%; 7% in mathematics to 61%.

- Valencia received the first Leah Meyer Austin Award from Achieving the Dream for reducing targeted course completion gaps among students from different backgrounds while raising course completion of all students.

- Valencia was the 2012 winner and first recipient of the Aspen Prize for Community College Excellence based on its completion/transfer, learning, workforce, and equitability outcomes.

To specifically understand how students experience LifeMap, Valencia has been conducting student surveys and focus groups and analyzing students' use of the My LifeMap tools since 2001.

LifeMap Surveys

Online surveys were conducted with students in 2001 and 2004 and with faculty in 2002 and 2004. (Selected results are summarized in Table 3.1.) Students were asked about their education planning behavior and then asked specifically what they knew about LifeMap. In both surveys, a majority of students indicated that they did have an education goal (91% and 96%), whereas only about half indicated that it was "written down." Students' awareness of LifeMap, however, showed a marked change between 2001 and 2004: The percentages of students who said they had heard of LifeMap and could provide a description of it increased from 53% to 83% and 20% to 58% respectively. This increase indicated that Valencia could teach the majority of its students to understand the program and led it to market the LifeMap concept throughout the college.

Table 3.1 ◆ Student and Faculty Awareness of LifeMap

Survey Items	% Responding	
Students	**2001**	**2004**
Had an education goal	91%	96%
Had a written education goal	46%	51%
Heard of LifeMap	53%	87%
Able to provide written description of LifeMap	20%	58%
Faculty	**2002**	**2004**
Thought learning goals important for students	90%	98%
Thought career goals important for students	63%	72%
Discussed goal-setting with students outside class	86%	72%
Could tell students a few things about LifeMap	45%	40%
Could explain to students how LifeMap worked	49%	21%

In both 2002 and 2004, a large majority of faculty agreed that it was important that students have well-defined learning and career goals. Faculty awareness of LifeMap, however, appeared not only to be low in 2001 but to decrease in 2004. Whereas the percentage of faculty who could tell students a few things about LifeMap decreased slightly (45% to 40%), the percentage indicating that they could explain to students how LifeMap worked, decreased sharply (49% to 21%). Analysis revealed several factors affecting the results. In 2001 only full-time faculty were surveyed, whereas in 2004 adjunct faculty were also surveyed. Also, the 2001 survey followed more closely after the August 2000 rollout of the first LifeMap marketing campaign that was actively supported by the president and academic administration as a new college initiative. Since that time, Valencia has worked to create more continuous faculty induction programs that integrate LifeMap into the regular college culture.

My LifeMap Tool Use

Since Atlas was introduced in 2002, Valencia has tracked students' use of the My LifeMap tools. As mentioned earlier, groups convene annually to discuss the use and evolution of each tool. The 2011 annual report indicated the following cumulative usage statistics for LifeMap tools.

- My Education Plan: 21,000 plans developed; 117,000 saved.

- Me in the Making: used by more than 21,000 students.

- My Career Planner: used by more than 2,500 students.

- My Job Prospects: used by almost 1,000 students.

- My Financial Planner: used by more than 1,000 students.

- My Portfolio: more than 900 portfolios created.

To focus further on the use of My Education Plan, the cornerstone of LifeMap, Valencia developed analytical reports to understand correlations between students' education plans and academic behavior. One report allows comparison by term of the number of students with new education plans and the percentage of those plans that match the program of study entered in the system (based on their application or update form submitted to the college). Students can create and save up to three program plans in My Education Plan, but one is indicated as their primary. Although Valencia has seen an increase in the match between what is recorded in My Education Plan and the system, it is still a relatively low alignment. In fall 2005, there were 2,912 new education plans, and 18% matched the students' recorded program of study. In fall 2011, there were 9,515 new education plans, and 43% matched the program of study. It appears that students are entering one thing on their applications but developing different education plans, perhaps as they learn more about the programs available at Valencia.

Another report includes the number and percentage of students each term who have an education plan and the percentage who are enrolled in courses that are in their primary education plan. Again, the correlations are increasing but are not as high as expected. In fall 2005, 45% of the enrolled students had an education plan, and 46% of them were enrolled in courses in their education plan. In fall 2011, 56% of the enrolled students had an education plan, and 61% of them were enrolled in courses in their education plan. These reports also provide student-level information so that Valencia can follow up with individual students who appear to be "off plan" to understand what their plans are and assist them to get on track. Further research is under development.

A third report compares the percentage of graduates who have education plans with the percentage who completed the degree designated in their primary education plan. In fall 2005, 34% of graduates had an education plan, and 21% graduated in the degree program that matched their primary education plan. In fall 2011, 60% of the graduates had an education plan, and 27% graduated in the designated degree program. This is another finding that bears further investigation. Our financial aid degree compliance procedures already notifies students by Atlas e-mail who are enrolled in courses that are noncompliant based on the degree program entered in the system, because financial aid cannot be awarded for these classes. These students typically then see an academic advisor or counselor who can review their plans with them and make adjustments to their program or course enrollment as needed.

Student Focus Groups

Valencia has conducted focus groups with students who do and do not have education plans to understand how they approach their program planning, what resources they use, and so on. Results have shown that students who have an education plan are using all of the planning tools—My Education Plan, the catalog, the student handbook, program planning sheets, and the Atlas degree audit—and then they want to talk to a person to make sure that what they understand about degree requirements is accurate. Because an early design principle was to enhance the advising conversations by giving students as much information as possible to research on their own before talking with an advisor or instructor, Valencia adopted the phrase "system working as designed!"

On the other hand, those students who did not have an education plan were not planning much at all. They were visiting the Answer Center sometime before classes started to find out what they needed to do next. These students seemed impressed by My Education Plan when it was reviewed in the focus groups, but it is not clear whether those students have increased their use of LifeMap tools. These are the students that Valencia continues to work with to encourage their developmental progress in taking ownership of their education and the resources available to them.

Student Learning Outcomes

Valencia has evaluated the learning outcomes of advising through a learning assessment survey conducted once or twice a year over multiple years. Students respond to six learning outcome statements immediately following an advising session. For example, over five administrations from 2007 to 2011, 76%–83% of students strongly agreed with this statement: "I have an improved understanding of the requirements needed to complete my degree/certificate." And 70%–72% of students strongly agreed with this statement: "I am able to make informed decisions about my education and career goals." This learning assessment is conducted, shared, and discussed by counselors who help each campus advising team shape its training and improved professional practice based on this student learning assessment. The learning outcomes of LifeMap have started to be evaluated through the work of Valencia's counselors as part of the faculty learning outcomes assessment at Valencia. The counselors have designed and implemented learning assessments of different general education program outcomes (e.g., critical thinking, ethical responsibility) by focusing on learning evidence from new student orientation, the academic suspension student readmission program, and the evaluation of education plans.

CONCLUSION

Many times Valencia has been asked how it has been able to implement such a comprehensive system as LifeMap. Was buy-in top down or bottom up? From the advantage of looking back over the years of development, I can share that it was honestly a collaborative effort driven by a common desire to improve students' success. It was surely the right combination of leadership and ownership from all parts of the college. We truly learned together, were driven by the literature and big ideas of what could be, and also referred to data and evidence to check our progress. We believe it is critical to have a conceptual model that is rooted in theory and research that serves as the foundation and reference point for the continuing development of the system. Throughout Valencia, we identify our big ideas of what improves student success and use these as a basis for directing our efforts and focus (Shugart, Puyana, Romano, Phelps, & Walter, 2011). We are always welcoming new students, faculty, and staff to our community, so we have to make sure we invite everyone in to participate and contribute. As we practice our big idea that "the college is what the students experience," we must ensure that LifeMap and Atlas (as well as the entire learning community) develop along a trajectory that authentically helps students achieve their goals, as that is the only thing that really matters.

REFERENCES

Frost, S. H. (1991). *Academic advising for student success: A system of shared responsibility* (ASHE-ERIC Higher Education Report No. 3). Washington, DC: George Washington University, School of Education and Human Development. (ERIC # ED340274)

Gordon, V., & Sears, S. (1997). *Academic alternatives: Exploration and decision-making*. Upper Saddle River, NJ: Gorsuch Scarisbrick.

Hammer, M., & Champy, J. (1993). *Reengineering the corporation*. New York: Harper Business.

Hammer, M., & Stanton, S. (1995). *The reengineering revolution: A handbook*. New York: Harper Business.

Hossler, D., & Schmidt, J. (1990, February). *Progress report: A longitudinal study of the postsecondary plans and activities of Indiana high school students*. Bloomington, IN: Indiana University.

Kilingman, P. D., Castellano, B., & Kelley, S. (2008). *Valencia community college: A history of an extraordinary learning community*. Orlando, FL: Valencia Community College.

O'Banion, T. (1994). An academic advising model. *NACADA Journal, 14*(2), 10–16.

O'Banion, T. (1997). *A learning college for the 21st century*. Phoenix: Oryx Press.

Shugart, S., Puyana, A., Romano, J., Phelps, J., & Walter, K. (2011). Valencia's big ideas: Sustaining authentic change through shared purpose and culture. In T. O'Banion & C. D. Wilson (Eds.), *Focus on learning: A learning college reader*. Phoenix, AZ: League for Innovation in the Community College.

Tinto, V. (1993). *Leaving college: Rethinking the causes and cures of student attrition (2nd ed.)* Chicago: University of Chicago.

Valencia College. (2013a). *2012–2013 LifeMap handbook/Planner*. Downloadable from http://valenciacollege.edu/studentdev/campusInformationServices.cfm

Valencia College. (2013b). *Faculty development*. Available from http://valenciacollege.edu/faculty/development/coursesResources/LifeMap.cfm

Valencia College. (2013c). *Student services: Skillshops* [Web page]. Available from http://valenciacollege.edu/studentservices/skillshops.cfm

CHAPTER 4

West Kentucky Community and Technical College: The Master Advising Center

Deborah Smith, S. Renea Akin, Sandra Tucker, and Sherry Anderson

West Kentucky Community and Technical College (WKCTC) is located in Paducah, Kentucky, on a 216-acre campus in the far western part of the commonwealth. It serves a 10-county area and enrolls more than 9,000 students per year. The college, part of the Kentucky Community and Technical College System, offers not only traditional 2-year associate degrees in arts or sciences designed for transfer, but also associate degrees in fine arts and applied science, along with diplomas and certificates in several technical fields. As a comprehensive community college, WKCTC is committed to providing high-quality educational experiences, meeting the education needs of the college community, serving as a full partner in business and workforce development, and contributing to the overall economic and social well-being of the region. As a result of offering a variety of programs and course delivery options, and due to the diligent efforts of the faculty and staff, in 2011 the college was named by the Aspen Institute as one of the top five community colleges in the nation.

PRIOR TO 2002, MOST ACADEMIC advising at West Kentucky Community and Technical College (WKCTC) took place using an arena-style registration process that was focused primarily on helping students create a schedule of classes as quickly as possible. With the selection of a new president and in light of other organizational changes, including a merger that effectively doubled the number of students in need of advising, WKCTC made a commitment in 2002 to transform its academic advising program to better meet the needs of the students. The goal was to move away from advising that simply assisted students in putting together a class schedule to a model that actively supported teaching and learning. To fulfill this commitment, the college began by bringing in a higher education consultant, Jerry Hinton of Hinton and Associates, to review existing processes and offer suggestions for improvement. Hinton recommended that the advising center undergo a massive restructure and begin providing proactive and Web-based orientation, advisement, career/education planning, assessment and placement, and an early alert/referral system to front-load success and remove barriers for students.

Hinton's recommendations, coupled with a review of relevant documents including Vincent Tinto's *Leaving College* (1993) and Hunter Boylan's *What Works* (2002), formed the basis for the development of the master advising center. In 2005, following extensive remodeling to convert former office space into a comprehensive academic advising center that includes a reception area and a combination of private offices for professional academic advisors and eight workstations equipped with computers and printing capability for faculty advising, the college launched the master advising center to support WKCTC's strategic goal to "promote excellence in teaching and learning."

During this same period, the college made a commitment to move all student services such as financial aid, the registrar's office, and business services to a single location—the Anderson Technical Building—to create a one-stop shop for students. With the relocation of the college bookstore and TRIO student support services in 2011 and placement of an intake coordinator in the lobby of the Anderson Technical Building, WKCTC achieved its goal. As a result, new and returning students are now able to enroll at the college, complete placement testing (if needed), meet with an advisor and a financial aid counselor, pay their fees, and purchase their books in a single location. Josh Wyner, executive director of the Aspen Institute, noted that WKCTC's implementation of the one-stop shop removes a roadblock to student success by enabling students to take care of all registration needs in one place instead of "wandering around campus."

Processes in the master advising center were further refined in 2008 after the college asked Hunter Boylan, director of the National Center for Developmental Education, to conduct a comprehensive assessment of the developmental education program at WKCTC. This consultation was made possible by a Title III-HEA grant. Through the use of Title III resources and with administrative support, a concerted effort began to improve developmental education outcomes across the campus, including advising for students underprepared for the academic rigors of college.

The college established an academic support program, which later became the Council for College Readiness, to develop a plan to implement Boylan's recommendations and better meet the needs of the college's underprepared students. The plan included the use of strategies such as supplemental instruction, targeted advising, expanded tutoring services, curriculum revision, technology-mediated instruction, and professional development for faculty, staff, advisors, and tutors to address the remediation needs of students. Boylan also recommended that the college explore the extent of misplacement in developmental and gateway courses, add a measurement of students' noncognitive characteristics to the existing assessment battery, and train academic advisors to be more aggressive in planning programs, schedules, and activities for underprepared students.

MISSION AND GOALS

Academic advising in the 2-year college setting is challenging due to the heterogeneity of the student body, the variety and complexity of decisions students must make, and the frequent need for developmental programs of study to prepare students for collegiate work. WKCTC strives to meet the needs of its student body, which varies widely in academic potential and academic interest. The mission of the master advising center is to provide accessible, innovative, and comprehensive advising services within an environment of excellence and commitment to student success. The center accomplishes its mission by providing and coordinating undergraduate and transfer advising services, providing professional development to faculty advisors, coordinating student placement and assessment services, monitoring student progression, and providing students with services such as transfer fairs to facilitate transfer.

REPORTING STRUCTURE

WKCTC's advising program is supportive of the general philosophy of an open access college: to assist individuals, through college programs, to realize their full potential as educated citizens. At WKCTC, academic advising is a multifaceted, institutionwide effort aimed at providing advising services to support the teaching and learning process and to assist students to meet their academic and career goals. As will be described later, advising is a joint effort between faculty and staff in the areas of student affairs, academic affairs, and learning initiatives. The shared structure employed by WKCTC is similar to the split model described by Pardee (2004).

The master advising center is staffed with five full-time, professional advisors. In 2011, the ratio of students to professional student services staff in the area of counseling and advising was in the 96th percentile nationwide according to results from the National Community College Benchmark Project. All professional advisors are trained and prepared to provide comprehensive advising for all programs and transfer pathways offered at WKCTC. One advisor, a content expert in transfer requirements, serves as the coordinator of transfer advising. The center provides dedicated space to allow advisors from regional institutions to maintain a regular physical presence on campus to assist students with transfer decisions and planning. The director of the master advising center reports directly to the vice president of student affairs and supervises the staff of the assessment center, the unit that conducts all placement testing.

The vice president of student affairs also employs three recruiters who travel to area high schools to meet with students, provide academic and career counseling, and assist students with developing a schedule and registering for classes. The recruiters work closely with the master advising center staff. As noted earlier, the college has placed an intake coordinator in the lobby of the building that houses all student services. As an admissions advisor, the intake coordinator provides prospective and new students with the initial guidance needed to begin the application, assessment, and enrollment processes. The intake coordinator also provides career and program information and general information about applying for financial aid. The goal of this office is to have new students ready to focus on academic advising when they enter the center. The intake coordinator is a unit of the admissions and records office and is supervised by the director of admissions/registrar, who in turn, reports to the vice president of student affairs.

The bulk of academic advising at WKCTC is a joint effort of the master advising center staff and full-time faculty whose job description includes advising students. Advising is an important component of faculty responsibilities. The quality and effectiveness of faculty advising activities are considered for progress toward promotion and tenure and factor into the annual performance review for all full-time faculty members. Faculty fulfill their academic advising obligations by working directly with assigned advisees and by working with unassigned advisees in the center a set number of hours each academic year. Staffing of the master advising center is supplemented in summer months by full-time faculty who are compensated for their time. Faculty who work in the center during the summer months are considered master advisors through a combination of professional development, experience, and the desire to work with students in this capacity. Staffing the center with teaching faculty ensures students have ongoing contact with experienced faculty advisors throughout the year. Faculty typically report to an academic dean; the academic deans report to the vice president of academic affairs.

Other areas under the direction of the vice president of academic affairs that play a role in advising include veterans services, a student success coach, and a workforce transitions coordinator. Veterans services is led by a coordinator who advises veterans and assists them with financial aid, veterans benefits, academic advising, and career counseling. The student success coach advises dislocated workers and assists them with developing an academic plan, financial aid, career counseling, tutoring, and locating other resources as needed. The workforce transitions coordinator advises students who have completed college credit through workforce training to assist them with the college admission process, assessment preparation, academic planning, and making connections with other resources as needed.

The vice president of learning initiatives is responsible for a number of college functions, including distance learning, institutional research, and professional development. The college employs a full-time director of online student services who provides complete advising services to students enrolled in online courses. The director of online student services works closely with the director of advising to ensure that students who are enrolled only in online classes receive advising services that are comparable to the advising services offered to students enrolled in traditional classes.

Collaboration and communication are key components of the college's advising program. Effective partnerships between academic affairs, student affairs, and other student support units have enabled the college to be creative and flexible in developing an academic advising program that integrates many campus resources to meet students' education needs.

ACADEMIC ADVISING FROM INTAKE TO DEGREE COMPLETION

Students who step onto campus for the first time are greeted by an intake coordinator, whose office is located at the entrance of the building in which all student services are housed. The intake coordinator is an admissions advisor who provides prospective and new students with the initial guidance needed to begin the application, assessment, and enrollment process. Prospective students who have not completed the college's application may do so at a kiosk located within sight of the intake coordinator. The intake coordinator also provides career and program information and general information about applying for financial aid.

A checklist for new students is provided to recently admitted and prospective students to assist them in navigating the admissions and registration process. The goal of the intake office is to prepare new students so that they will be ready to focus on advising and be ready to enroll in classes by the time they reach the master advising center. WKCTC students are required to meet minimum placement scores to ensure their preparedness for the academic rigors of college course work. Students whose ACT scores are below the minimum required for enrollment into entry-level courses are required to take the COMPASS placement assessment. To facilitate student success and accuracy of placement as suggested by the college's consultant, Hunter Boylan, students complete an orientation prior to testing. This orientation is designed to introduce students to the purpose of placement testing and provide an overview of the online COMPASS placement assessment. Following the orientation, students have three options: Students who are ready may choose to take the placement test at the conclusion of the orientation, students may choose to test at a later date after reviewing a study guide provided by the assessment center, or students may choose to participate in COMPASS preparation sessions at the WKCTC adult basic education center.

After completing the COMPASS placement test, students meet with a post-assessment advisor. Students who wish to repeat COMPASS may be referred to the college's academic support center (formerly known as the tutoring center) or to the WKCTC adult basic education center, which is located in the same building. Students who do not wish to retest are referred to the master advising center. Testing results are immediately available to advisors. Advisors incorporate assessment results in the advising process to ensure accurate placement in courses and facilitate student success.

Data indicate that students who participate in remediation prior to retesting fare better than those who simply wait thirty days and retest. These results demonstrate the importance and effectiveness of advising and guidance through the assessment and placement process. As with the admissions counselor in the intake office, the advisors in the assessment center provide an important link in the overall advising process that increases the likelihood that students are well-prepared before they enter the master advising center.

All new students are required to meet with an advisor in the master advising center when enrolling for the first time or when returning to college after a break in enrollment. To ensure adequate time for advising, new, prospective, and returning students are encouraged to schedule appointments with center advisors. During the first few weeks of the term, students are assigned a faculty advisor based on their declared major or program of study. Recognizing the necessity of tailoring advising to individual needs, advisors are assigned to students in a systematic process based on academic preparedness and program plan.

Undecided students are assigned to the professional advisors in the center. Students enrolled in two or more developmental courses are assigned to faculty in the transition (developmental) education division or to other individually selected advisors who understand the unique needs of students who test into developmental classes. Students who qualify for TRIO student support services are assigned to TRIO advisors. All others are assigned to faculty advisors based on major or program plan of study. This system pairs students with advisors who are experts in particular areas through background experience, personal interest, or professional development.

Advising appointments are booked in 1-hour increments to allow adequate time for advisors to develop a quality advising relationship and help students make a personal connection with the college. Advisors are prepared to discuss programs and majors, program requirements, and course selection and to refer students to other campus resources as needed. Students who have selected a major are provided with an academic plan outlining the courses required for credential completion, while undecided students are referred to the office of career services where they are given the tools needed to explore a variety of career options.

Students who are unsure about a career path are encouraged to complete the online FOCUS 2 program, a self-paced, online career guidance tool that assists students in self-assessment and career exploration and is intended to help students choose a major and make informed decisions about their careers. The master advising center began using the original FOCUS in 2006. In spring 2007, letters were mailed to 247 students whose majors were listed as undecided. Each student was given a FOCUS password and instructions for accessing the program. By June 2007, 94 students had used the program. Advisors can use the assessment results to help match students with career options and majors and programs.

One of the first steps taken by the master advising center staff when WKCTC committed to redesigning its advising process was to work with the academic program coordinators to publish academic plans for each degree, diploma, and certificate on the college's website. Publishing the first academic plans, and subsequently keeping them all current, has been no easy task considering that WKCTC offers more than 400 credentials. Taking this step, however, has been crucial to the success the master advising center has had in enabling faculty advisors to advise students more easily and accurately in academic areas in which the faculty member may have no personal experience, since these plans include both a list of courses needed to complete each credential and a suggested course sequence. The course sequence is helpful in identifying potential advising hazards such as prerequisites and courses that are not offered each semester. College-specific academic plans allow the college to differentiate WKCTC course and program offerings from the courses and programs included in the systemwide catalog, which includes courses and programs offered at all KCTCS institutions and which can be a source of confusion for students, faculty, and staff. In addition to providing counselors and faculty with current information, the academic plans enable students to take responsibility for understanding which courses are required for their programs of study. Academic plans are posted online and are updated regularly. Having easy online access to this information has enhanced the advising program for counselors, faculty, and students.

When developing an academic advising plan, counselors and faculty take into consideration each student's academic history. Both ACT and COMPASS scores are available to counselors, faculty, and admitted students electronically via the PeopleSoft student information system, which may be accessed from any computer with an active Internet connection. This system also provides access to advanced placement credit, transfer equivalency course work, credit for prior learning experience, and military credit. The system provides counselors and faculty advisors with access to students' completed and in-progress course work, cumulative grade point average (GPA), grades, credentials awarded, major, and academic plans. Counselors and faculty advisors also have access in PeopleSoft to the student's record of completion of a required on-campus or online new student orientation. Students may enroll in courses for one semester without completing this orientation but may not enroll in subsequent semesters without completing this academic requirement. Counselors and faculty advisors are able to stress with students the importance of completing this orientation (Boyd, Largent, & Rondeau, 2008).

All nursing and allied health programs at WKCTC use objective admission criteria in which points are awarded for factors such as grades in specific courses, overall GPA, ACT and SAT scores, etc., to select students for admission. Because the selective admission criteria for each program vary according to the needs of the program, center advisors are provided with an overview of the admission requirements for each program. Selective admission criteria are also available on each program's Web page. In order to be considered for admission to one of these programs, students are required to attend a pre-admission conference. These conferences are led by the coordinators of each program a minimum of four times during each application cycle. The pre-admission conference is a form of academic advising that takes place in a group session to ensure that all students interested in nursing and allied health are provided with the information necessary for them to be well prepared for the selective admission process and for the requirements of the related career. From 2002 to the present, academic advising at WKCTC has evolved from a culture of schedule building to a culture of providing comprehensive advising services grounded in teaching and learning that foster personal growth and a sense of responsibility for academic and career goals.

NEW FACULTY/ADVISOR ORIENTATION TO THE COLLEGE

All new faculty and staff participate in a first-year experience orientation program. This program consists of shared faculty/staff experiences and includes a full-day orientation followed by monthly meetings designed to build camaraderie and provide focused training on specific areas of the college such as public relations, professional development opportunities, and student services. In addition, all new faculty participate in additional orientation activities, including an overview of advising intended to provide faculty with the basic skills needed to advise students using the curriculum guides published for each academic program.

Because the advising needs of students in different academic programs vary, new faculty are assigned mentors within their academic division and spend time shadowing experienced faculty advisors in the center. This allows the new faculty advisor to become better acquainted with the specific advising needs of the students in the academic area in which they teach. For example, although all faculty advisors are able to use the published curriculum guides to advise students in an allied health or nursing academic program, a faculty advisor who teaches in this area will be able to share personal experiences in the clinical setting with students to help them decide whether they are pursuing the appropriate career path. Likewise, faculty advisors in areas such as science and mathematics can more readily help students align course requirements for the associate degree with those for the bachelor's degree. The mentoring program enables experienced faculty to share this type of knowledge, which is difficult to quantify. All faculty advisors annually participate in required professional development provided by advising center staff to alert faculty to any changes in the advising process. Survey results for 2008–2010 reveal that 90%–96% of faculty strongly agree or agree that advising workshops improve their knowledge of the advising process.

New professional advisors, who are classified as staff, also participate in the first-year experience program. These advisors are closely mentored during the first 3–6 months of employment. Training, orientation, and mentoring are tailored to fit individual needs, depending on level of experience and familiarity with the institution. All center advisors and staff participate in workshops provided by the office of academic affairs each year or on an as-needed basis. These training workshops are used to introduce changes and revisions in curricula and program requirements.

Students evaluate advisors and counselors each fall using a common instrument. Faculty advisors, the vice president of academic affairs, and the deans of each academic division receive copies of faculty advisor results. Faculty establish performance goals each year pertaining to advising, and those who fail to meet their set goals meet with their dean to develop a performance improvement plan. The institutional research office creates a summary of all student evaluation of advising results that is shared internally on the college's Intranet.

SPECIAL FEATURES

Advising Undecided Students

Because research shows that students tend to be more successful and will complete a credential sooner if they have a clear goal in mind, staff in the center work intensively with students to reduce the number without a declared major (Lewallen, 1993). Center advisors meet with returning undecided students, for example, and discuss education and career options to help them make informed decisions and develop long-term academic plans. Advisors assist students with gathering information about careers and transfer options and integrating the information into educational choices. As a result of these efforts, significant numbers of previously undecided students have declared a major (see Table 4.1).

Table 4.1 ◆ Reduction in Number of Undecided Students at West Kentucky Community and Technical College

Academic Year	# of Undecided Students		% Reduction
	Fall	Spring	
2010–2011	364	177	51%
2009–2010	348	184	47%
2008–2009	185	134	27%

Degree Audits

WKCTC has been tracking student completion as part of its strategic planning process since 2006. IPEDS graduation rates increased from 31% in 2007 to 39% in 2010. National Community College Benchmark Project results reveal that while the percentage of full-time WKCTC students who completed a degree or certificate or transferred within 3 years increased from 32.8% in 2007 to 37.5% in 2010 (94th percentile), the most significant increase came from part-time students whose credential completion or transfer rates increased from 29.5% in 2007 to 35.1% in 2010 (98th percentile). Several factors contribute to student success in this area, including degree audits by staff in the center. Each semester, the advisors evaluate the transcripts of all students who were enrolled the prior semester, did not complete a credential, remain in good academic standing, and did not return the following semester. Students who have completed a credential are notified and encouraged to apply for graduation. Other students who are near completion are encouraged to return to college. Degree audits conducted during the spring 2012 semester indicated that 99 students had earned but not received a credential during the previous semester.

Academic Coaching

In spring 2011, the associate vice president of academic affairs, in collaboration with the director of advising and assessment, secured a grant to fund a pilot academic coaching project targeted at providing additional support for students enrolled in two or more developmental courses. Accurate assessment, effective academic advising, and appropriate placement are critical components of successful developmental education programs (Boylan, 2002; McCabe, 2000; Morante, 1989). The academic coaching project involved staff and faculty from the assessment center, master advising center, adult basic education, and the transition (developmental) education division and all students enrolled in GEN 102, Foundations of Learning. GEN 102 presents strategies that promote academic and personal success in college, including using campus resources; focusing on learning and memory, critical reading and thinking, classroom skills, and time management; and allowing for career exploration. All students enrolled in GEN 102 participated in the pilot project as a component of the course.

At the beginning of the semester, students completed a noncognitive learning styles assessment and were assigned an academic coach. Center staff served as the academic coaches for this project. During the second week of the semester, students were required to meet with their academic coaches to review the results of the noncognitive assessment and develop an action plan for improvement in areas of deficiency. The assessment included interest in learning, responsibility, adapting to change, teamwork skills, problem solving, and persistence. Course requirements included meeting with the assigned coach a minimum of three.times during the semester. Coaches maintained regular contact with students via e-mail, text messaging, or phone, depending on the students' preferences.

Students were required to write a reflection paper describing the experience; other assignments included visiting key offices or departments on campus and gathering information about the services these units provide. Since students who need support services the most are often the least likely to seek them out on their own, these assignments served as a proactive means of introducing students to valuable resources (McCabe, 2000). One problem reported early in the project by the academic coaches was limited student involvement, even though participation was linked to the course grade.

First-Year College and Transfer Focus

WKCTC is currently participating in two initiatives of the John N. Gardner Institute for Excellence in Undergraduate Education's Foundation of Excellence:

(1) First College Year and (2) Transfer Focus. Both include a thorough self-study of the college as it serves and supports transfer-bound students and those aspects of the new student experience. As a result of this evaluation process, action plans have been developed that include creating an advising council. This council will include faculty and student services staff. The charge of this council will be to support the role of faculty in the advising program and serve as a bridge between academic affairs and student affairs. The council will assist in coordinating faculty advising and professional development for faculty advisors and will take a lead in new initiatives related to the advising program at WKCTC.

USE OF TECHNOLOGY

WKCTC uses multiple forms of technology across campus to ensure that students, faculty, and staff have access on the college's website to the tools needed to support an effective academic advising program. For instance, students have online access to the admission application, placement assessment requirements, program descriptions, selective admission criteria for specific programs, academic plans, course schedule, FOCUS 2, and the required college orientation program. Students' use of technology begins with the application process since even new students who are physically on campus complete the application online at a kiosk in the lobby of the student services building.

As previously noted, ACT, COMPASS, and advanced placement scores are entered in the PeopleSoft student information system, which also includes transfer equivalency course work, credit for prior learning experience, military credits, completed and in-progress course work, grades, credentials awarded, and major and academic plans. PeopleSoft is also the platform that provides counselors, faculty advisors, and currently enrolled students with online access to information. Links to the 24/7 student self-service resource provided through PeopleSoft are posted on the college website. After completing the college application, students are assigned an ID number that is used to create a PeopleSoft account. Students are able to view their class schedules, make a payment, change an address or phone number, view their degree progress report, locate their advisor's contact information, and even register online for classes. Online registration is not available for new students; only returning students in good academic standing are given self-enrollment permission. Students also have access to an electronic, searchable schedule of courses. The course schedule is updated daily to reflect the most current course information. Classes may be accessed by subject area, location, and time. Online classes may be accessed separately from on-campus classes.

The WKCTC website also includes information and links for students planning to transfer. Links to KnowHow2GoKY, Kentucky Transfer Handbook, and Transfer Evaluation System provide advisors and students with current information about transfer to 4-year institutions, including course equivalencies and articulation agreements. Students who are unsure about a career path are provided access to the online FOCUS 2 program described earlier. Internally, the advising center uses an online calendar to easily schedule and share information about advising appointments. Each counselor and the center's administrative assistant have access to the calendars. The system is also used to track the number of appointments and times when additional help is needed in the center.

SPECIAL FUNDING

The vice president of academic affairs provides funding from the part-time faculty budget for full-time faculty to work in the advising center during the summer. This commitment to the advising program was made when the program was developed and has continued to provide support to the center. In addition, the student success coach position is funded by a KCTCS Trade Adjustment Assistance Community College and Career Training grant; the workforce transitions coordinator position is funded by KCTCS as part of a systemwide initiative to transition workforce development students into academic programs.

PROGRAM EVALUATION

As part of WKCTC's annual institutional assessment process, the master advising center engages in ongoing and systematic assessment to measure its performance. The institutional assessment process includes establishing outcomes and targets, evaluating results and data, and using results for improvement. Each fall, the master advising center reviews its findings for its achievement targets established the previous year to identify areas of success as well as areas that need improvement. Action plans are developed when targets are not met. The program also reviews its mission and outcomes for continuation or revision and revises achievement targets as needed. The college uses an online assessment management system that allows for immediate sharing of assessment results with relevant parties. The master advising center's assessment results are accessible to the vice presidents of student affairs, academic affairs, and learning initiatives, and to the associate vice president of learning initiatives, who is responsible for institutional planning, research, and effectiveness. Each year, a summary of all institutional assessment results is shared internally on the college's Intranet.

The center's assessment plan includes outcomes to improve unit processes, student satisfaction with services, and institutional targets. For instance, in 2008 center staff began contacting students, who left the college in good standing after completing a minimum of 12 credit hours, to encourage these students to return. Since initiating this process, yield rates have increased from 12% in spring 2009 to 22% in spring 2011. After realizing that wait times for walk-in students at the master advising center often exceeded an hour during peak enrollment periods, the center worked with the vice president of academic affairs to institute changes: Faculty are asked to commit 4 hours per semester during peak enrollment periods, which has enabled the center to handle more effectively the increase in student volume and reduce the wait time. Students are asked to complete an exit survey when they apply for a credential. The master advising center monitors results for two questions on this survey. From 2009 to 2011, 95%–96% of students who completed the survey expressed satisfaction with advising services, while 98%–99% reported satisfaction with placement testing services.

To support the college's retention and graduation targets defined in the WKCTC Strategic Plan, when 2009 institutional data indicated an increase in the number of students without a declared major, master advising center staff began an initiative to reach out to those undecided students and assist them in gathering information that would aid them in making a decision about a possible major. As a result of this intervention, the percentage of credential-seeking students identified as undecided during their first semester decreased by 27% in 2008–2009, 47%

in 2009–2010, and 51% in 2010–2011. The office of institutional research provides online reports to the master advising center to support advising services. An example of these reports is a list of students who were enrolled, did not complete a degree, and did not return the following semester.

CONCLUSION

We believe the advising program at WKCTC is exemplary and of value to other community colleges for the following reasons:

◆ The advising program is a collegewide initiative designed to fully support student learning and success by ensuring that students are in the classes they are prepared for and are not taking unnecessary courses.

◆ Student evaluations indicate a strong satisfaction with the advising services offered.

◆ Targeted outreach efforts such as contacting students who have not returned to college have resulted in improvements in enrollment.

◆ Concentrated advising for undecided students has significantly reduced the number of students without a declared major, which—while difficult to quantify—has no doubt contributed to improvements in retention.

◆ WKCTC's transfer rate in 2009 was 26.8%, the third highest in the commonwealth. Transfer success is related to local partnerships with institutions such as the University of Kentucky, which offers bachelor of science degrees in engineering on the WKCTC campus and statewide transfer agreements, staffs the master advising center with a full-time advisor who is a content expert in transfer advising, and provides dedicated space to allow advisors from regional institutions to maintain a regular physical presence on campus to assist students with transfer decisions. As Murray State University is WKCTC's top receiving institution, the center staff and departmental faculty maintain a close working relationship with the education, business, nursing, and information systems departments at Murray. Representatives from each institution meet periodically to review the impact curricula changes at either institution will have on students who are transferring.

We believe the greatest challenges that other colleges will face in implementing this program are as follows:

- Organizing and coordinating the multiple aspects of the program across the lines of division that traditionally exist within many colleges.

- Recognizing the value of strong student support services as they relate to retention and success.

- Recognizing that efforts to increase enrollment alone do little to ensure persistence and success.

- Involving faculty in the advising process.

- Providing training for new faculty and ongoing professional development for all faculty and staff.

- Maintaining accurate curriculum guides when curricula change frequently at both the local college and institutions to which students transfer.

- Developing and maintaining working partnerships with other colleges and universities.

REFERENCES

Boyd, B., Largent, L., & Rondeau, S. (2008). *Community college orientation basics: How to structure a new student orientation program.* Retrieved from http://www.nacada.ksu.edu/Clearinghouse/AdvisingIssues/Orientation.htm

Boylan, H. R. (2002). *What works: Research-based best practices in developmental education.* Boone, NC: National Center for Developmental Education.

Lewallen, W. C. (1993). The impact of being "undecided" on college student persistence. *Journal of College Student Development, 34,* 103–112.

McCabe, R. H. (2000). *No one to waste: A report to public decision-makers and community college leaders.* Washington, DC: Community College Press.

Morante, E. A. (1989). Selecting tests and placing students. *Journal of Developmental Education, 13*(2), 2–6.

Pardee, C. F. (2004). *Organizational structures for advising.* Retrieved from http://www.nacada.ksu.edu/clearinghouse/AdvisingIssues/org.models.htm

Tinto, V. (1993). *Leaving college: Rethinking the causes and cures of student attrition* (2nd ed.). Chicago: University of Chicago Press.

CHAPTER 5

William Rainey Harper College: Student Advising Through the Life Cycle

Sheryl M. Otto,
Eric Rosenthal, and
Joan L. Kindle

William Rainey Harper College, established in 1965, is located in the northwest suburbs of Chicago, with the main campus in Palatine and two nearby extension centers. Harper College is a comprehensive community college with annual enrollments of more than 28,000 for-credit students. The student population is diverse, with over 35% students of color and 39% over age 25. Approximately 50% of credit students plan to transfer to a 4-year institution, 20% plan to pursue career programs, and the remaining students seek to enhance their skills and knowledge for professional or personal growth. Named for the first president of the University of Chicago, who was a pioneer in the junior college movement, the college is fully accredited by the Higher Learning Commission of the North Central Association of Colleges and Secondary Schools.

In keeping with the national completion agenda set by President Obama, Harper College's goal is to graduate an additional 10,604 students between 2009 and 2020. This focus has been institutionalized via the college's strategic plan, outlined in nine goals and enacted by action teams. Five of the goals have particular relevance to the student success initiatives reviewed in this chapter: (1) creating stackable career and academic pathways that incorporate industry-relevant and postsecondary credentials that lead to a sustainable income, (2) ensuring P–20 curriculum alignment and transfer articulation, (3) decreasing student achievement gaps of underprepared, young male, and Black non-Hispanic students, while increasing academic achievement for all, (4) increasing the percentage of first-time, full-time freshmen from feeder high school districts who begin in credit-bearing courses, and (5) increasing the number of certificate and degree completers.

EDUCATION REFORM IS FRONT AND center on the national agenda. An issue reaching crisis proportions is the lack of degree completion. Although access to college has increased with undergraduate enrollment doubling between 1970 and 2009, the rate of degree completion has not increased (Complete College America, 2011). In stark contrast to the stalling graduation rates is the rising number of jobs requiring postsecondary credentials. "By 2018, more than 63 percent of prime-age workers will need some type of postsecondary instruction... [and] the postsecondary system will have produced 3 million fewer college graduates than demanded by the labor market" (Carnevale, Smith, & Strohl, 2010, pp. 13–15). President Barack Obama (2009) specifically asked community colleges to create "programs that track student progress inside and outside the classroom. Let's figure out what's keeping students from crossing that finish line, and then put in place reforms that will remove those barriers" (p. 4).

William Rainey Harper College (Harper College) has responded to the national student success agenda and developed systemic processes that engage students through improved academic advising and tracking systems. Aligning newer integrative approaches to the student experience with collaborative services (see, e.g., Jenkins, 2007; Myran, 2009), Harper College has widened its approach with a student flow model from admissions to graduation. The focus diverts from the role of the administrative unit and instead centers on the continuum of the student experience with an integrated collegewide response system.

This chapter will highlight the academic advising model embedded into the student experience at the college. It should be noted that Harper College has adopted a student success agenda within a 5-year strategic plan aimed at actively exploring and launching initiatives that support greater student achievement and completion rates. To this end, the entire college is moving toward more integrated, comprehensive approaches to student success. Along with the description of the academic advising model, it is necessary to include the integrated systems within which it coexists. Additionally, it is recognized that the systems are part of a continuous improvement process that has and will continue to adjust based on evaluative data.

Access to success serves as the central mission of Harper College's advising model. Success services throughout the student life cycle include the on-boarding process, interventions for at-risk students, and ongoing student support and the use of technology to expand accessibility with self-service options. Aligned with the strategic plan to integrate approaches and widen the net of support, the expansion of partnerships with educational systems, on both secondary and university levels, is reviewed later in the chapter. Also, an accounting of a variety of programmatic supports is provided, including professional development, program evaluation and outcomes, and resources. The chapter concludes with an overview of emerging practices.

FOUNDATIONS OF THE HARPER COLLEGE MODEL

Playing a major role in Harper College's mission, the student development division has a 30-year tradition of providing holistic academic, career, and personal advising to students in the context of highly effective success programs offered in various modalities. The division was built on the premise that academic advising infused with counseling provides the most effective structure to support the whole student. As is depicted in Figure 5.1, academic advising is offered within six student development service areas; other services are also provided but are unique to each center and are not duplicated (e.g., resumé assistance is provided only in the career center). While each student development center has a unique primary mission catering to specific student populations, all the centers are unified through the infused academic advising-counseling philosophy and function as an integrated whole.

This centralized yet decentralized organizational structure for academic advising is supported by 17 full-time and 18 part-time master's-level professional counselors who provide the holistic advising. Counselors are assigned to work in a specific center but may assist in other centers during peak periods or during the summer. Students who opt to receive advising in one of these areas can develop a home base where they receive several touches of support from one counselor. For example, a student in the career center may receive career counseling and assessment as well as course advising from a counselor; a student using the center for multicultural learning may receive academic advising from the counselor who also serves as the student club advisor to the Black Student Union to which the student belongs. Each of the student development centers is led by a director or

Figure 5.1 ◆ **Structure of the Harper College Academic Advising Model**

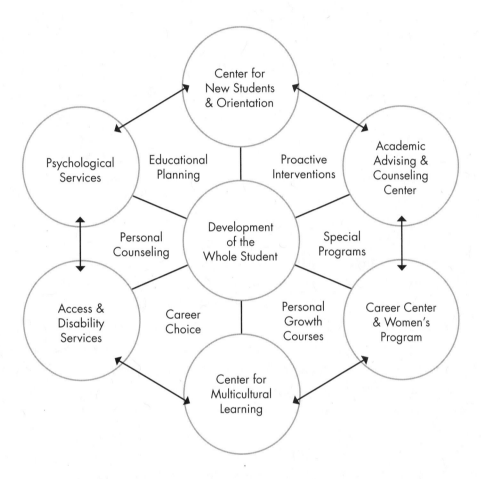

associate dean reporting to the dean of student development. The dean reports to the college provost who in turn reports to the college president.

In addition to providing traditional one-on-one and small-group advising, student development also offers credit courses (e.g., First-Year Experience, Career Development, Humanistic Psychology, Exploring Diversity in the U.S., Topics in Psychology) and special programs to support student achievement. Critical to the model are several professional staff members other than counselors who also provide advising-related information, either by gathering and disseminating it or directly presenting it to students in individual and group formats. The role of student leaders has been vital as well, with new student orientation facilitated in part by student orientation leaders and peer mentors providing valuable assistance to at-risk students in programs designed to maximize their success and personal growth.

The Student Personnel Point of View, created by the American Council on Education in 1937 and revised in 1949, provided a historic foundation that has been at the center of the academic advising philosophy at Harper College. Students are seen as whole people who have needs to develop "physically, socially, emotionally, spiritually, as well as intellectually" (Williamson et al., 1949, p. 2). Students play an active and accountable role in their own development. A state of maturity cannot be reached unless all aspects of one's persona are attended to in an integrated manner.

The academic advising model at Harper College strives to create a systematic yet personalized advising approach that begins upon entry and provides various touch points and safety nets within the student life cycle (see Table 5.1). The model is purposefully designed to avoid turning the open door into a revolving door. It continues to evolve with a shifting emphasis from merely providing opportunities for access to higher education to a more systemic and intrusive program that aids students in their goal completion. While the approaches have varied over the years to better meet demands and the needs of changing student demographics, the advising program has never lost sight of the individual student. A hallmark of the model has been a personalized approach to meet students where they are upon entry to the college, to continue to monitor their progress in meeting key milestones, and to intervene with differing levels of support based on their unique needs so that they may ultimately be successful in reaching their goals.

THE ON-BOARDING PROCESS

The first stage in the student life cycle is focused on transition and engagement. Mandatory assessment and orientation for new full-time students have been a part of the academic advising program at Harper College since the mid-1980s. New full-time students are assessed in basic skills (reading, writing, and mathematics) using ACT's COMPASS test. Data are collected on key attrition characteristics such as past academic performance, ethnicity, first-generation status, and hours

Table 5.1 ◆ Advising Touch Points Throughout the Student Life Cycle

Student Life Cycle	Advising Touch Points
On-boarding	• Orientation • Basic skills assessment • At-risk determination • Summer Bridge • Tailored first semester schedule
0–15 credit hours	• FYE 101 course • Early alert • Individualized success plans
16–30 credit hours	• Career development course • Degree audits • Educational plan to goal completion
31–45 credit hours	• Mandatory advising for probation • Transfer advising and college fair
46–60 credit hours	• Graduation checks • Job fair and resumé • Required course for suspension
Degree completion	• Career and transfer graduate surveys
Alumni	• Job search assistance • Career change support

devoted to work and other outside commitments. Information is used by counselors and students during orientation to make informed first-semester enrollment decisions. Underprepared students may be directed to an additional 2-week summer college preparatory experience or various developmental sequences offered during the first semester; high-achieving students are directed to opportunities for honors course work; and undecided students are presented with the option to enroll in a career development course taught by a counselor. Persistence rates for students participating in the 2-day assessment and orientation were 99% for semester retention rates and 93% for persistence to the next semester.

Harper College has noted that students who enter underprepared have a high risk of not completing their academic goals. To increase college readiness, emphasis has been placed on early transition for developmental students through summer bridge programs. The REACH Summer Bridge targets underprepared and underrepresented students with two or more developmental placements. The program assists with both academic preparation and connections with counselors in the center for multicultural learning. Retention, persistence, and success rates for participants have been positive. Comparisons to similar students not participating in REACH are noted in Table 5.2. Recently, the college has taken a closer look at its on-boarding experience and is making revisions to the new student flow process from recruitment through the first semester (see Table 5.3). Policy changes and process improvements that are components of this redesign will include (a) adding part-time, degree-seeking students into the mandatory assessment and orientation process; (b) creating more tailored new student orientation, advising, and registration pathways based on a student's intended goal; (c) providing an additional noncognitive assessment tool; and (d) enforcing first-semester enrollment in developmental course work for students identified as not college ready.

Table 5.2 ◆ Success Rates for REACH Summer Bridge Students

Success Measure	REACH Students	non-REACH Students
Semester retention	97%	86%
Persistence to next semester	84%	77%
Semester GPA 2.0 or higher	72%	45%

SUPPORT FOR AT-RISK STUDENTS

Advising plays a pivotal role in several interventions designed to assist students most at risk for having academic difficulty. To address students' needs and also to help students already struggling to get back on track, programs have been put in place at various stages of students' experiences. The ultimate goal is to set students on early pathways to success and reduce the number of students in need of interventions.

Beginning immediately in their first semester, Project Success provides at-risk students the opportunity to receive early interventions. The program, piloted in fall 2011, is part of the collegewide student success plan as well as the national Achieving the Dream: Community Colleges Count (ATD) initiative in which Harper College participates. In keeping with ATD's culture of evidence, the

Table 5.3 ◆ **On-Boarding Process for New Degree-Seeking Students**

Activities and Milestones	Outcomes and Goals
Phase 1: Recruitment	
• High School: early planning, dual credit, concurrent enrollment, open houses. • Young Adult/Adult Population: fast track, information sessions, open houses. • Limited Enrollment: information sessions.	Application generated.
Phase 2: Application	
• Academic Goal/Program of Study: associate, transfer, certificate, fast track, student at large, concurrent/dual enrollment, credit. • Start Date: fall/spring/summer; summer only (at large). • Application Status: full time/part time. • Other: AP/CLEP, high school transcript, COMPASS, transfer credit, financial aid, testing.	Screening process complete.
Phase 3: Testing	
• COMPASS Testing: High school, new students. • Other: ACT, AP/CLEP credit, transfer credit. • Interpreting Scores: Study aides, retesting.	College readiness determined.
Phase 4: Orientation, Initial Advising, and Registration	
• Identification of Special Populations: Summer Bridge, disabilities, athletes, distinguished scholars. • System Navigation • First Semester Schedule Building: success seminar, accelerated, initiatives, developmental education, learning communities. • Tuition/Fees	Registration process complete.
Phase 5: First Semester Support	
• Student Success Seminar • Mentoring • Education Planning to Goal Completion: degree plan and audit, transfer advising, accommodation plan, career exploration and counseling, portfolio development. • Monitoring at-Risk Students: early alert, financial aid, academic standing.	First semester complete.

college determined that students placing into two or more developmental courses or a sequence of developmental courses are significantly less likely to succeed and continue to enroll. Entering students with such characteristics are selected to participate in the program.

Participating students are targeted for intervention if instructors detect signs of academic difficulty. This is facilitated by the implementation of the Starfish Early Alert software system, allowing instructors to respond quickly to online surveys sent between the 4th and 6th weeks of the semester. Poorly performing students are electronically flagged, assigned a counselor, and contacted to make an appointment. The process is facilitated by the project success specialist.

During the advising appointments, the counselor and the student collaborate to develop an individualized success contract designed to increase the student's ability to reach academic goals, aided by an extensive intake form. To ensure standardized interventions, counselors receive comprehensive training on Starfish to manage their caseloads and advising strategies especially salient to at-risk students. Ongoing communication among faculty, counselors, the project success specialist, students, and referral resources (e.g., tutoring center) occur via Starfish.

Outcomes for the pilot were exceptionally positive, largely attributable to high rates of participation by faculty and students alike. Of 278 full-time and adjunct faculty asked to provide feedback about their students' performance, including raising flags as needed, 191 (69%) participated. Of the 335 students in the initial cohort, 189 (56%) were flagged by instructors, with 145 (77%) of these flagged students meeting with a counselor. Outcomes indicate higher success and persistence rates for students who met with a counselor (see Table 5.4).

Students who continue to struggle after their first semester enter Harper College's Standards of Academic Performance (SOAP) system, established in 1989. This comprehensive and intrusive advising program is designed to identify students who are having academic difficulty and provide academic support to maximize their success. Facilitated by the Banner student information system (SIS), the SOAP process involves several potential stages (see Table 5.5). These are not intended to be punitive but rather offer a structured approach for various levels of intervention to be enacted (voluntary to mandatory).

Table 5.4 ◆ Success Rates for Project Success Students

| | Counseling Status | |
Success Measure	Counselor flagged, seen	Counselor flagged, not seen
Persistence to next semester	82%	48%
Grade C or better in all courses	59%	29%
Grade C or better in developmental courses	59%	32%

Table 5.5 ◆ Stages of the SOAP Intrusive Advising Process

SOAP Status	Criteria	Success Strategies
Caution	Attempted 7+ credit hours and cumulative GPA less than 2.0.	Caution letter recommending success-oriented strategies, including an interactive web-based success intervention.
Warning	Attempted 16 or more credit hours with cumulative GPA less than 2.0, or second successive semester with cumulative GPA less than 2.0.	Warning letter recommending success-oriented strategies and restriction to maximum 13 credit hours.
Probation	Previous semester with academic warning and cumulative GPA less than 2.0.	Mandatory restriction to maximum of 13 credit hours. Required success-oriented strategies including meeting with a counselor.
Suspension	Attempted 40 or more credit hours, at least three successive semesters with cumulative GPA less than 2.0 with one of those terms in probation, and earned below a 2.0 semester GPA the last semester enrolled.	One semester suspension with opportunities to use advising services. Required success-oriented strategies upon return, including meeting with a counselor.
Post-Suspension	Semester after suspension and subsequent semesters with semester GPA of 2.0 or higher and cumulative GPA of less than 2.0.	Mandatory restriction to maximum of 13 credit hours. Required success-oriented strategies, including meeting with a counselor.
Dismissal	One semester after suspension or a previous semester in post-dismissal with semester and cumulative GPA less than 2.0.	Dismissal for two semesters with opportunities to use advising services. Must petition for reinstatement.
Post-Dismissal	Semester after reinstatement from dismissal and subsequent semesters with semester GPA of 2.0 or higher and cumulative GPA of less than 2.0.	Mandatory restriction to maximum of 13 credit hours. Required success-oriented strategies, including meeting with a counselor.

Table 5.6 ◆ Success Rates for Students With SOAP Probation Status Receiving Advising

Success Measure	With Advising	Without Advising
Semester retention	94%	78%
Persistence to next semester	81%	36%
Semester GPA 2.0 or higher	58%	40%

Counselors draw upon their professional skills to help SOAP students identify past and future obstacles to success, build concrete strategies for academic improvement, and develop and apply personal strengths. Students are required to take Gallup's Strengths Finder assessment, which identifies their talents and suggests ways to build and apply them in academic, career, and other key areas. Students are assisted primarily via individual sessions, but over 100 probationary students each year participate in SOAP groups, which involve a 1-hour group session followed by individual advising. The format is cost-effective and allows students to benefit from other students' experiences. Student success outcomes for SOAP are positive with higher retention, persistence, and achievement (see Table 5.6).

Should students progress to academic suspension and be granted an appeal by the dean, they may be required to enroll in a specialized success course taught by a counselor. In this humanistic psychology course all students take the Strengths Finder assessment and receive strengths-infused instruction and individual counseling and advising. Students are also paired with peer mentors (developmental advocates) based on similar and complementary strengths, and mentors are trained to assist students using a strengths-based approach. Academic progress has been noted by students participating in the developmental advocates success course: From an average beginning GPA of 1.62, the average after the success course was 2.91.

In response to new federal regulations, counselors are playing a larger role in assisting students with financial aid issues. With financial aid threatened, students are at even greater risk in achieving their academic goals. Academic plans are developed to help students return to compliance with federal Satisfactory Academic Progress rules, affording the opportunity to continue their studies and eventually earn the desired credential.

ROLE OF TECHNOLOGY

Technology is a vital component of Harper College's academic advising model infrastructure. Within the student development advising centers, technology provides tools ranging from electronic calendars and appointment books to online records of educational planning sessions with students. Harper College has increasingly used technology to improve accessibility and provide students with more self-service advising options. Technological advances have afforded new ways to communicate with students about their academic progress, resulting in more earned credentials.

Technology is embedded throughout Harper College's advising model and facilitates a variety of daily activities. SARS·GRID, an appointment scheduling software package, is used in each student development advising center. Reports from the software provide data about numbers of students being served, appointment cancellation and show rates, and traffic patterns across advising centers. Administrators use the software to make informed staffing decisions and to gather figures for program evaluation. Counselors make extensive use of the SIS when working with advisees. The SIS allows counselors to identify vital information about students, including academic history prior to and during enrollment at Harper College. A customized student composite report has been developed to consolidate into a single resource SIS information most frequently used by counselors. The report has reduced the amount of time spent searching for data, thereby allowing counselors to spend more time engaging with students.

Student progress toward degrees or certificates is tracked via the degree audit system, a tool used frequently in the context of advising. Detailed educational planning notes provided to students are scanned and indexed to their SIS records, making this documentation available to counselors in all student development advising centers. The SIS is also an integral component of the SOAP program. As the end-of-semester academic status is calculated for students, the SIS places registration holds and credit hour restrictions on probation students. As counselors meet with the probation students, the registration holds are lifted and the recommended success strategies are recorded in the SIS, allowing student compliance over time to be tracked.

The development in 2009 of a My Advising tab on the student portal greatly enhanced the provision of advising information to students by creating a single, organized online resource for them (see Figure 5.2). My Advising has high rates of use, particularly during peak registration periods. Via several portal channels, the following are easily accessible in the My Advising tab:

- Answers to frequently asked advising questions. Students with additional questions can select a link to ask a counselor a quick question, or students can email their questions directly to a counselor with whom they have been working.

- Academic record information. Students have easy access to calculating their grade point averages and viewing their grades or unofficial transcripts.

- Degree and certificate evaluations. Electronic degree audits allow students to track their progress toward degree or certificate completion and to perform what-if scenarios as they explore different programs of study. Students can also track progress with respect to 4-year degrees at institutions participating in u.Select, an online system detailing transferability of Harper College courses and their applicability to university graduation requirements.

- Transfer information. "Major guides" that outline sample two-year course plans are available for students who know they want to transfer in a particular area of study, but are not certain of their transfer school. Additionally, transfer school-specific guides and articulation agreements are accessible online so that students can make informed course selection decisions when transfer destination schools are already known.

- Advising news. Updated weekly, students see announcements about upcoming events (e.g., transfer fairs and college visits), receive reminders about important advising and registration dates, and obtain success tips such as academic success strategies.

- Online workshops and other helpful resources. Links to individual advising centers and other academic support service areas (e.g., access and disability services, tutoring center) are centrally provided along with links to online workshops covering a variety of academic, career, and personal development topics (e.g., building your strengths, anti-procrastination strategies). A comprehensive online tutorial guides students in course selection and registration processes.

Figure 5.2 ◆ Illustration of the My Advising Student Portal Tab

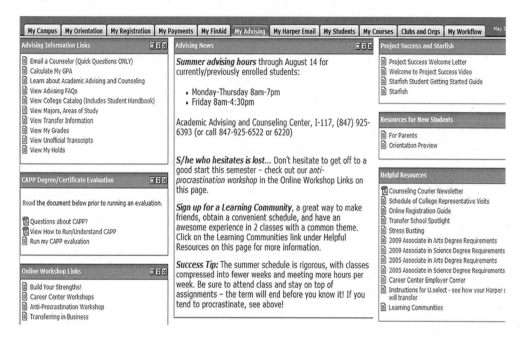

Technology also plays a significant role in an initiative designed to assist students in crossing the finish line. The completion concierge approach involves contacting students who are close to earning a credential. Students receive a degree audit outlining unmet requirements and are encouraged to enroll in the courses needed to complete their degrees or certificates. Students are provided a special phone number and contact person to assist them. Referrals are made to academic advising for assistance with course selection if needed. In four semesters, over 2,000 additional credentials were awarded (see Figure 5.3).

Figure 5.3 ◆ **Impact of Use of the Completion Concierge on Credential Increase**

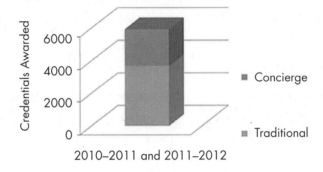

PARTNERSHIPS: WIDENING THE NET OF SUPPORT

With recognition that the student experience flows naturally within and outside of the classroom, collaborations between teaching faculty and support services staff as well as partnerships that align success efforts with other education systems have been targeted to strengthen Harper College's advising model. The Association of American Colleges and Universities (AACU) and the Carnegie Foundation for the Advancement of Teaching promote the importance of integrative learning practices for all students in order for them to be better prepared to succeed in a diverse, interconnected world (AACU & Carnegie Foundation, 2004). Integrated learning includes interconnections among academic disciplines and includes co-curricular experiences. Harper College endeavors to ensure student success by collaborating with other institutions to foster seamless transitions. This before-and-after approach benefits students as they enter the college as well as when they progress to 4-year colleges and universities.

Teaching Faculty and Support Service Staff Collaboration

Collaboration with teaching faculty has been a fundamental practice within the advising program at Harper College. Each academic program has a counselor liaison who works with the academic department chair to provide updated information on program requirements as well as career and transfer options. Faculty and counselors often participate jointly in outreach efforts and information sessions designed to give students and parents pertinent information about particular areas of study, such as a recent collaboration to design an improved system for allied health career program information sessions. Counselors train academic department chairs in how to use degree audits to provide students with information about their degree or certificate progress, and to analyze enrollment patterns for planning future course schedules.

The counselor–faculty relationship extends beyond programmatic exchanges. Today's community college students are faced with myriad issues that can be barriers to their success, requiring faculty to provide students with more than instruction. Counselors have been instrumental in helping teaching faculty to better understand the complexities of today's students and how to improve support in and out of the classroom. Counselors provide training for faculty on creating accessible classrooms, managing disruptive student behaviors, and increasing diversity awareness. There are fellowships for faculty who want to delve more deeply into multiculturalism, preventing domestic violence, or infusing principles of Universal Design for Learning. Select faculty fellows are trained through the student development division to infuse these topical areas into their curricula. Fellows share their infusion projects with other faculty during faculty orientation week held prior to the start of the semester. To date, 59 faculty representing all academic divisions have completed a fellowship.

Also illustrating the synergy between student development and teaching faculty are Harper College's REACH Summer Bridge and early alert programs for at-risk students, involving coordinated interventions by counselors and faculty. Counselors are also invited into faculty classrooms to address special student needs—an ideal way to integrate academic and student services. In 2011 advising personnel made 115 in-class presentations on psychosocial and life management topics reaching 2,117 students. Examples of in-class presentation topics are as follows:

- academic success strategies

- building your strengths

- bystander intervention

- career exploration

- diversity awareness (several topics)

- math confidence

- registration and transfer basics

- self responsibility and plagiarism

- sexual assault prevention

- stress management

- time management/overcoming procrastination

- transferring in business

Learning outcomes are determined in advance of the classroom presentations by counselors, and self-assessments are completed by students. Classroom outcomes were rated highly by students. For example, in one assessment 97%–98% agreed or strongly agreed that they had a greater understanding of their unique strengths and those of others and that they could use their strengths to be successful in the course.

Secondary School and College Partnerships for College Readiness

About 1.62 million high school students took the ACT assessment test in 2011, the instrument used to assess students' college readiness in accordance with benchmarks in four subject areas: English, reading, mathematics, and science. One in four met all four college-readiness benchmarks, and 28% met none of them (ACT, 2011). ACT reported that test scores have remained static between 2007 and 2011 even though 25% more students were tested. It is common practice to blame high schools for these rates of failure, but it is more effective for colleges to work with high schools to change practices that will lead to improved rates of college-ready students. (Alliance for Excellent Education, 2011; Bolden, 2009; Collins, 2009; Conley, 2010; Templin, 2011).

To create sound partnerships with area high schools, Harper College established a formal intergovernmental agency in 2010 with its three high school districts (12 high schools) called the Northwest Educational Council for Student Success (council). Formal, board-approved memorandums of understanding affirmed the council's established goals, which include the following:

- Ensure curriculum alignment.

- Increase the percentage of first-time new students who begin in credit-bearing courses.

- Identify funding and leverage partner resources for innovative projects.

- Create stackable career and academic pathways that incorporate industry-relevant and postsecondary credentials.

The council began its work with an examination of students exiting high school needing developmental mathematics upon entry at Harper College. Data indicated that about 56% of the entering students fell into this category. The council also determined that students who ended with Algebra II in their junior year in high school and did not take senior year math were at higher risk for placing into developmental math. Completion rates of degree-seeking students who enter in developmental mathematics were alarmingly low.

Through collaborative efforts between the high schools and Harper College, the council launched an initiative to increase the percentage of first-time, full-time students beginning in college-level math courses. Typically, Harper College students who need developmental mathematics are identified using the COMPASS assessment upon entry. The council decided to identify students in need of mathematics intervention before the senior year of high school. The result was a joint high school–community college project, aptly named Partners for Success—Mathematics, which includes five components:

- Mandate COMPASS testing of high school juniors.

- Encourage juniors to take math their senior year.

- Align high school Algebra II and Harper College's Intermediate Algebra courses.

- Identify multiple methods to qualify for college credit mathematics.

- Offer dual credit general education mathematics as a senior year math option.

Harper College assisted with establishing systems and protocols for COMPASS testing in the high schools. High school and Harper College faculty collaborated on curriculum alignment, standards, and assessment measures. The efforts of the partnership have begun to make a positive difference in student achievement, as noted by the results in 2011 from one district that piloted the project. Outcomes compared to the previous year include

◆ 8% increase in enrollment in senior math by Algebra II juniors.

◆ 6% increase in the number of Harper College first-year students taking college-level math.

◆ 11% decrease in the number of Harper College first-year students taking the lowest level developmental math course.

Early COMPASS testing and curriculum alignment projects enhance the academic advising process by allowing greater opportunity for more students to enter college-ready and also for more information sharing about the needs of students upon entry. The partnership has been successful in establishing trust among staff in high schools and the college, enhancing the understanding of the different systems of the partners, and sharing data. The partnership will continue to schedule regular meetings and plans to expand programs and practices to ensure student success.

PARTNERSHIPS WITH TRANSFER INSTITUTIONS

Harper College students benefit from more than 100 articulation agreements allowing seamless transfer to 4-year institutions. The transfer coordinator and director of academic advising and counseling leads counselors, academic faculty, and deans in the creation of partnerships with baccalaureate colleges and universities. A growing focus is the development of dual-degree partnerships with institutions to which students frequently transfer. The partnerships provide benefits for students expressing an early intent to transfer to participating institutions. Benefits include locked-in degree requirements, financial incentives such as scholarships and tuition discounts, and joint advising. Even more notable is a program that guarantees admission to the University of Illinois at Urbana-Champaign's highly ranked College of Engineering for entering students that meet academic requirements as they progress through the Harper College curriculum. These agreements encourage students to complete their associate degree prior to transfer but also provide means for students to "reverse articulate" credits should they find it advantageous to transfer without the Harper College degree, in order to earn the associate degree post transfer.

Although the development of such partnerships is a critical component, the students' and counselors' awareness of them is equally important. This is facilitated by the dissemination of transfer information by the transfer information specialist, whose primary responsibility is to organize the information and create effective means of communicating it to counselors and students. This is chiefly accomplished via well-organized online resources utilized widely by counselors and students alike. Frequent and timely e-mails, meeting updates, and in-service trainings are additional mechanisms by which counselors obtain key information. The transfer coordinator role is incorporated into the responsibilities of the director of academic advising and counseling, organizationally creating a seamless connection between the development of transfer partnerships and counselor use of this information to guide students toward successful transfer and eventual baccalaureate degree completion. Such partnerships are communicated to high school counselors to share with students, providing clear pathway options to postsecondary education.

PROGRAM SUPPORT

Professional Development

To ensure the quality of the various programs offered, professional development is a key element. Student development provides counselors with a comprehensive 8-week professional development program, supplemented by additional training in advising for special populations. The training curriculum is designed to equip counselors with knowledge, skills, and attitudes focused on the holistic needs of students. The program incorporates the key informational, relational, and conceptual components outlined by Habley (1995) in approximately equal proportions. Habley wrote that "without understanding (conceptual elements), there is no context for the delivery of services. Without information, there is no substance to advising. And, without personal skills (relational), the quality of the advisee/ advisor relationship is left to chance" (p. 76). To illustrate, understanding Harper

College programs and degrees and interpreting degree audits are informational topics, explaining degree audits to students and working with at-risk students involve relational skills, and conceptual issues include effective documentation and risk management. Coordinated by the director of academic advising and counseling, the content is provided via a team approach, led by a counselor who serves as the primary trainer but including segments presented by approximately 15 other professionals.

Several key experiential components such as case studies, practice and homework, and taking placement exams are employed to make the training hands-on and active. Over the 8 weeks, trainees progress from observing advising sessions, to being observed by a seasoned counselor as they take the lead with students and then debrief, to ultimately advising students on their own and consulting as needed. The rate of progress a counselor makes may vary depending on the trainee's prior experience; in this way, the training is customized to the needs of the individual. In all cases, these experiential modes are interspersed with content presented in didactic and discussion formats as well as desk time, allowing trainees to absorb and quickly apply new learning.

Beyond the training designed for new counselors, all receive ongoing training during their first year and in subsequent years. This includes a full-day in-service "update training" each semester that includes informational, relational, and conceptual components. There are also several other training opportunities provided each year, with recent topics including advising students with autism spectrum disorders, crisis intervention and suicide prevention, a diversity series, transfer advising for complicated majors, and understanding the needs of returning combat veterans. Both full-time and part-time counselors are given financial support for professional development such as workshop or conference attendance.

The training program is assessed in several ways. Trainees complete an evaluation form rating the overall effectiveness of the program and its components. They have consistently endorsed ratings of "effective" or "very effective." The program's success is also reflected in appraisals of the trainees' attainment of desired outcomes, namely their possession of the intended knowledge, skills, and attitudes. This multifaceted evaluation process incorporates input from several sources and perspectives, including the counselors who have observed the trainee advising students, as well as the primary trainer and assigned mentor. The trainee's own sense of progress and comfort level in advancing to the next level of training are also given significant credence.

All of this input is consolidated by the director of academic advising and counseling who, after incorporating his own observations, makes the ultimate decision regarding the trainee's readiness. Importantly, assessment is ongoing even after the new counselor is "cleared" to meet alone with students, with several sources available to identify areas calling for informal feedback. These sources include the counselor's contributions during meetings and other discussions and, when necessary, mentor review of educational planning documents. The director also directly observes counselors as part of annual performance appraisals. Student evaluations are also obtained, which recently showed nearly 100% of students expressing satisfaction with their counselors. Harper College's training program has been named as an exemplary practice in advising administration in the National Academic Advising Association monograph *Academic Advising Administration: Essential Knowledge and Skills for the 21st Century* (Joslin & Markee, 2011).

Program Evaluation

Several methods are used to evaluate the effectiveness of Harper College's advising program, with most assessments conducted on an ongoing basis. Examples of primary measures include the following.

◆ As key indicators of both demand and the capacity to meet it, the number of student contacts and headcount of students served are tracked every year. Each advising service area, such as the academic advising and counseling center or the career center, compiles data annually on the number of students seen for different types of services. Each area typically has between 12,000 and 17,000 duplicated student–counselor contacts per year, with an additional 3,000 to 10,000 contacts via in-class presentations, workshops, and outreach events. Prior year comparisons to numbers served and costs per contacts are conducted to identify trends. Both contacts and headcounts of student users have increased steadily each year, with an overall increase in the past 10 years that has outpaced an enrollment growth of about 12% over the same period.

- Point-of-service surveys, collected in each advising area, assess student satisfaction and learning outcomes. Survey responses reveal consistently high satisfaction with advising services (95%+) and similarly high agreement with learning outcome items such as, "I have a better sense of being able to succeed in my classes," "I know what steps to follow to transfer to another school," and "I have more information about how to get my certificate/degree."

- Student success indicators defined as retention, semester-to-semester persistence, and GPA are obtained on a consistent basis for populations being served by specific intervention programs (e.g., REACH Summer Bridge). Typical results have been shared earlier in this chapter with most data presented in aggregate, representing several years of research over the past decade.

Results of the measures just cited are analyzed and interpreted each year by service area administrators and institutional research staff and are summarized in end-of-year reports. The reports include planning for the upcoming year(s) based on this information toward a goal of continual improvement. Comprehensive 5-year program reviews involving full-day site visits by counselor and administrator colleagues from other institutions are also conducted, with results similarly used to generate plans to strengthen programs. Both types of reports are disseminated to counselors and other staff in the areas to which they pertain, and are also submitted to the dean of student development and the provost.

RESOURCES

Rising costs, growing enrollments, and shrinking state-supported funds require community colleges to be creative stewards of their resources. Programs that can demonstrate measurable outcomes will have an advantage in the competition for funding. Seeking opportunities to utilize internal and external funding sources that align with the national student success agenda can be supportive.

As part of its 5-year strategic plan, Harper College has committed $2 million for research, development, and piloting of strategic initiatives that directly impact student achievement and completion rates. Additionally, the college is dedicated to increasing student success by strengthening its efforts in grant writing and through strong support from the college's foundation. Such support helped to develop and launch several advising program initiatives. Both Project Success (Early Alert) and the developmental advocates program for students attending on an appealed academic suspension or dismissal got their starts through this type of support.

EMERGING PRACTICES

Harper College is a comprehensive community college offering a multitude of certificate programs and seven associate degrees with options including transfer curriculum, career and technical education, adult enrichment classes, and customized business training. An underlying tenet of academic advising at Harper College has been respect for student choice. Students are presented with an array of information about programs of study to explore from their point of entry. Whether this open structure of vast options is in the best interest of the typical community college is currently being examined. Navigating through the myriad options can be overwhelming for students (Jenkins, 2011; Scott-Clayton, 2011). More recent assessments indicate that "finding a path to degree completion is the equivalent of navigating a river on a dark night" (Scott-Clayton, p. 1). When students are less familiar with the college milieu and college expectations, it is more challenging for them to make sound decisions and achieve their goals (Brock, 2010; Conley, 2010; Karp, 2011). First-generation college students unfamiliar with the culture of college are often overwhelmed with all the options college offers (Scott-Clayton, 2011). In addition, research by Jenkins (2011), from Columbia University's Community College Research Center, indicates that entering a program of study within the first year of college increases the likelihood of earning a credential compared with students who entered a program of study in their second year. This research prompted recommendations to redesign college-wide processes to accelerate students' readiness and likelihood of selecting a program of study in the first year and moving to completion. These emergent recommendations and others have encouraged Harper College to look at a redesign of processes that focus on a more consistent structure and early decision-making for students.

Partnering for early decision-making, Harper College counselors have begun to offer "career liftoff" workshops for high school juniors and seniors who are undecided about a career or major. Students are invited to campus for a 2-hour interactive session to help narrow choices. Harper College has purchased the same career exploration software used in district high schools so students can smoothly transition career portfolios.

A more structured and consistent model for on-boarding and support through the first year will begin in fall 2013. All degree-seeking students, not just those who are full-time, will be required to take assessment exams as part of the orientation experience. Students who cannot demonstrate ability at college-ready levels in reading, writing, or math will be required to enroll in at least one developmental course each semester until the requirement is fulfilled. The comprehensive assessment will also evaluate students' academic, motivational, financial, social, career development, and support needs. Tailored orientation, advising, and registration pathways based on a student's intended goal will be offered.

During orientation, all degree-seeking students will select a contextualized student success seminar aligned with career or personal interests. The required seminar will serve as an anchor from which earlier and more robust career and academic planning will take place. The credit-bearing seminar will be taught by faculty across campus with a supportive counselor linked to each. The more comprehensive assessment of students will allow for the creation of a profile of each student's characteristics, skills, competencies, prior experience, educational and career intent, and goals. Using this profile, students and seminar-assigned counselors will jointly develop an individual education and career success plan (ECSP) to guide their pathway through the college experience. The ECSP outlines the academic pathway for achieving entry into a career or further education for students planning to transfer to a 4-year institution or who are stacking credentials into a career pathway. Poorly performing students identified through early alert will receive further intervention by the seminar-linked counselor with whom a relationship has already been built. With acquired success strategies and a roadmap in hand, as the seminar experience concludes, students may select a mentor for ongoing guidance.

To facilitate the more robust career and academic planning, Harper College will create an online environment to bring students' assessment profile, ECSP, e-portfolio, and other resources together in a single, easily accessible virtual location.

Students as well as faculty, counselors, and staff within the student's circle of support will be able to monitor and revise plans as needed. Dynamic prompts and personalized messaging will keep students on track to reaching key milestones on the path to completion.

Harper College is currently exploring how physical space can facilitate students' awareness and use of services. Plans are underway for a new one-stop admissions and student center. A more centralized academic advising model is being explored within the context of a larger, integrated service delivery system. A critical outcome will be to create a more intuitive, engaging, and infused support system into the student life cycle.

CONCLUSION

A vital key to an effective academic advising model is an integrated approach that embeds the service within the student experience. Similar to other college services for students, academic advising in community colleges has historically been available to those who voluntarily seek it, but many use it sporadically and some not at all. Students know that their class schedule is part of their academic experience, but services are often seen as auxiliary to their student life cycle. The organizational structure of most colleges encourages this view of the academic life separated from the services. The result is that, too often, advising services are accessible for those who are seeking help, but those who need it most fail to seek assistance. Many students do not adequately engage with the campus and persistence weakens. Academic services must meet the students at the front door not only to greet them but also to actively engage them with services and with people who can mentor and intervene as needed throughout the student life cycle.

With interactive and proactive approaches, academic advising must become part of the student flow from entry to exit. This integrated approach is an ongoing process and involves a student-centered focus across the college. Tinto (1993) expanded upon his seminal work on involvement theory by stressing that institutional commitment to students must be campuswide. "It is a pattern of activity that develops among all faculty and staff... It is a reflection of a campus-wide orientation to serve students that occurs in the various contexts in which students, faculty, and staff meet on a daily basis" (p. 149). Academic advising at Harper College is part of an integrated system that intentionally seeks in-class and out-of-class avenues for student engagement to occur. The goal is not for students to search for services but to be engaged to such a degree that the relationship is ongoing and the resources are part of the regular campus experience.

An important feature of the William Rainey Harper College model is that it is evolving. It is part of an intentional, active, and inclusive effort across the college to improve the student experience and support student success. Academic advising is expanding its reach through the college's partnerships with its high school districts and university articulation agreements; the expansion of summer bridge programs; its new policies on consistent student on-boarding experiences; the future development of a required success seminar for all degree-seeking students; the use of technology to enhance progress-tracking, interventions, as well as access to self-service; and the intentional efforts to bring academic instruction and important student support services closer together in collaboration around student success.

Harper College has not completed its work in creating student success opportunities for every student, and it may never finish this work. As articulated in the vision statement for the partnership between Harper College and its three high school districts, we are working to ensure that every high school and college graduate will have the opportunity to be prepared for 21st-century careers and postsecondary readiness and success. To that end, the academic advising program needs to continually evolve and improve its reach to all students by being open to new approaches and important collaborations and to be ever vigilant to ensure that success is possible for all students.

REFERENCES

ACT. (2011). *The condition of college and career readiness, 2011.* Retrieved from http://www.act.org/readiness/2011

Alliance for Excellent Education. (2011, May). *Saving now and saving later: How high school reform can reduce the nation's wasted remediation dollars* (Issue Brief). Retrieved from http://www.all4ed.org/files/SavingNowSavingLaterRemediation.pdf

Association of American Colleges and Universities & The Carnegie Foundation for the Advancement of Teaching. (2004, March). *A statement on integrative learning*. Retrieved from http://www.aacu.org/integrative_learning/pdfs/ILP_Statement.pdf

Bolden, J. (2009). Higher education access for underprepared students. In G. Myran (Ed.), *Reinventing the open door: Transformational strategies for community colleges* (pp. 33–43). Washington, DC: Community College Press.

Brock, T. (2010). Young adults and higher education: Barriers and breakthroughs to success. *Future of Children, 20*(1), 109–132.

Carnevale, A. P., Smith, N., & Strohl, J. (2010, June). *Help wanted: Projections of jobs and education requirements through 2018*. Retrieved from http://cew.georgetown.edu/jobs2018/

Collins, M. L. (2009, June). *Setting up success in developmental education: How state policy can help community colleges improve student outcomes* (Achieving the Dream Policy Brief). Retrieved from http://achievingthedream.org/sites/default/files/resources/SettingUpSuccessinDevelopmentalEducation.pdf

Complete College America. (2011).*The completion shortfall*. Retrieved from http://www.completecollege.org

Conley, D. T. (2010). *College and career ready*. San Francisco: Jossey-Bass.

Habley, W. R. (1995). Advisor training in the context of a teaching enhancement center. In R. E. Glennen and F. N. Vowell (Eds.), *Academic advising as a comprehensive campus process* (p. 76) (Monograph Series No. 2.). Manhattan, KS: NACADA.

Jenkins, D. (2007). Institutional effectiveness and student success: A study of high- and low-impact community colleges. *Community College Journal of Research and Practice, 31*, 945-962. doi: 10.1080/03601270701632057

Jenkins, D. (2011, April). *Get with the program: Accelerating community college students' entry into and completion of programs of study* (Working Paper No. 32). New York: Columbia University Teachers College, Community College Research Center. Available from the CCRC website: http://ccrc.tc.columbia.edu/ContentByType.asp?t=1

Joslin, J. E., & Markee, N. L. (2011). *Academic advising administration: Essential knowledge and skills for the 21st century* (Monograph No. 22). Manhattan, KS: NACADA.

Karp, M. M. (2011, February). *Toward a new understanding of non-academic student support: Four mechanisms encouraging positive student outcomes* (Working Paper No. 28). New York: Columbia University Teachers College, Community College Research Center. Available from the CCRC website: http://ccrc.tc.columbia.edu

Myran, G. (Ed.). (2009). *Reinventing the open door: Transformational strategies for community colleges.* Washington, DC: Community College Press.

Obama, B. H. (2009). *Remarks by the president on the American graduation initiative.* Speech presented at Macomb Community College, Warren, MI, July 14, 2009. Retrieved from http://www.whitehouse.gov/the_press_office/Remarks-by-the-President-on-the-American-Graduation-Initiative-in-Warren-MI/

Scott-Clayton, J. (2011). *The shapeless river: Does a lack of structure inhibit students' progress at community colleges?* (CCRC Working Paper No. 25). New York: Columbia University Teachers College, Community College Research Center. Retrieved from http://ccrc.tc.columbia.edu

Templin, B. (2011, Spring). America's community colleges: The key to the college completion challenge. *The Presidency.* Retrieved from http://www.acenet.edu/the-presidency/Pages/Spring-Supplement-2011.aspx

Tinto, V. (1993). *Leaving college: Rethinking the causes and cures of student attrition* (2nd ed.). Chicago: University of Chicago Press.

Williamson, E., et al. (1949). *The student personnel point of view.* Washington, DC: American Council on Education. Retrieved from http://www.naspa.org/pubs/files/StudAff_1949.pdf

CHAPTER 6

Indian River State College: Individualized Student Advising

Meredith Coughlin,
Dale Hayes, and
Steven Payne

Indian River State College (IRSC) transforms lives by offering high-quality, affordable education at five campuses on the east central coast of Florida. The college's continual evaluation and improvement of student services contributes to a high level of student success with increasing numbers of graduates and job placements in current and emerging careers. Centered on a 295-acre main campus featuring technologically sophisticated facilities, IRSC serves a four-county area with growing branch campuses in Indian River, Martin, Okeechobee, and St. Lucie counties. IRSC has taken the lead in helping the region transition into a diverse, knowledge-based economy, fueled by a highly skilled workforce.

IRSC partners with businesses, schools, universities, research institutes, hospitals, and government agencies to advance the educational and economic development of the region. The college's reputation for excellence attracts more than 32,000 students annually, with a 2011 FTE of 14,275. The college has experienced steady growth in the number of graduates with acceleration in the number of completers over the past five years.

I N APRIL 2007, INDIAN RIVER State College (IRSC) implemented a new academic advising program with newly admitted students. The goal is to ensure that every degree-seeking and dual-enrollment student benefits from a personalized, semester-by-semester program plan as a customized road map to graduation. Each degree-seeking student and dual-enrollment student is assigned a personal advisor. The formal notification of admission includes the advisor's name, e-mail address, and phone number. Prior to implementation of this program, all advising was completed on a walk-in basis with students often seeing different advisors with each visit. Student satisfaction surveys resulted in a common, recurring theme: Students were frustrated with long lines and disjointed services. In 2001, IRSC conducted a series of focus groups with students, administration, faculty, and staff to solicit feedback about student service activities and policies with the goal of improving delivery methods and—by extension—student success and satisfaction. Focus group participants suggested combining student services and moving toward a one-stop model.

The concept of a one-stop model required cross-training all student service staff. This training focused on a model in which one advisor assists a student from admissions through graduation. During one comprehensive meeting, the advisor assists the student with admissions, assessment and placement, financial aid, advising, and registration. The model is also designed to empower students to become more self-sufficient in the use of online student services. Advisors recognize that as students gravitate to online services there might be less and less contact, so advisors work hard to maintain personal contacts with their students.

IRSC organizes its student services within a single division under the umbrella of educational services. The educational services division is under the vice president of instructional services/main campus provost, who provides leadership to the branch campus provosts. This connection ensures that policies and practices are consistent across campuses. Educational services is organized around units of admissions and records, advising, assessment, career services, financial aid, veterans affairs, student disability services, and student success services. All of the above-mentioned services are provided at all campuses either by professional staff or through electronic access.

Unlike IRSC's advisors, student success staff do not have an assigned student caseload but are cross-trained in all education services functions and serve as the first point of contact for students entering the college. They are trained to assist students with any routine student services inquiry or need. For example, they assist students in completing the online admissions application and Free Application for Federal Student Aid, navigating course registration, using online resources, and accessing career services. In addition, each student success staff member facilitates a section of online new student orientation (NSO). They are responsible for monitoring each student's progress toward NSO completion and regularly contacting those students who may need additional assistance.

In addition to the student success services staff, there are 20 advisors across the five campuses who have an assigned caseload of students based on the students' selection of a "home" campus. Academic advising is coordinated by the chair of instructional advisement. The chair provides expertise in curriculum, evaluation, scheduling, and program planning. Additionally, the chair is responsible for the training of newly appointed advisors and reports to the associate dean of educational services.

PROGRAM MISSION

IRSC is making it personal—ensuring that every degree-seeking student has an individual advising plan (IAP) with ongoing encouragement from an assigned advisor from admission to graduation. The IAP maps out all courses required in a student's program of study in a suggested sequence by semester. Advisors guide students in their program choices, recommend resources for their needs, anticipate road blocks, and help the student navigate the pathway to success. Academic advising plays a vital role in increasing student retention (Dirr, 1999; Fishback, Kasworm, & Polson, 2002), and the IAP has become a critical step in helping students create a roadmap to keep them focused on their goals.

IRSC also assigns advisors to dual-enrollment students. These students, concurrently enrolled in high school and college courses, take general education courses to meet associate degree and high school diploma graduation requirements.

Dual-enrollment students are often not aware of how their courses apply toward an associate degree, and they can benefit from early interaction with an advisor through early career exploration and advice regarding college courses. Most area high school graduates take their first steps toward postsecondary education at IRSC. In fact, more than 70% of the region's college-bound high school seniors attend IRSC following graduation. Forty-four high school students earned their associate degrees at the time of high school graduation at the end of the 2009–2010 academic year; that number grew to 93 at the end of the 2011–2012 academic year.

PROGRAM MODEL

How well a college meets students' academic advising needs plays a vital part in minimizing student attrition (Noel, 1978). In spite of the importance of academic advising to student success, it is underutilized nationally. According to the Center for Community College Student Engagement (CCSSE), only 38% (27,936 of 73,406) of the students agreed or strongly agreed that an advisor helped them set academic goals and assisted in the creation of a plan for achieving them. Only 26% (19,085 of 73,488) indicated that someone talked to them about their outside commitments while helping them decide how many courses to take during their first term (CCSSE, 2012).

Research shows that student attrition can be attributed to myriad reasons, including financial hardship, lack of academic readiness, work or job conflicts, motivational issues, or lack of involvement with the institution (Astin, 1984; Ramist, 1981; Tinto, 1975). Habley, a leading authority on advising, reported similar reasons for student attrition and concluded, "One of the primary factors affecting college retention is the quality interaction a student has with a concerned person on campus" (2004, p. 16). Advisors are those concerned people and, as such, academic advising is a cornerstone of retention (Crockett, 1978; Cuseo, 2003; Glennen, 1996; Metzner, 1989; Tinto, 1999). Providing students with a personal advisor is IRSC's way of connecting students with a concerned person on campus. While negative academic advising experiences can result in students leaving the institution, positive experiences can lead to students investing more energy and effort in the college experience (Pascarella & Terenzini, 1991). Academic advising has an effect on student retention through increased student satisfaction, higher grades, and fewer departures (Metzner, 1989).

The relationship and interaction between advisor and student serve as a key form of student involvement (Ender, Winston, & Miller, 1982). Student involvement is defined as "energy devoted to the academic experience" (Astin, 1984, p. 297) where students' time is viewed as a resource that has to be allocated between multiple commitments. Advisors are faced with the challenge of finding a "hook to stimulate involvement" (Astin, 1984, p. 304) so that more time is allocated to institutional-related activities.

Leaders at IRSC reviewed the research on student success and began planning a new model of student services that would incorporate academic advising as the key to student success. The following questions provided a framework for exploring new models:

- What if we located student services all together in one place?

- What if each student was assigned a designated advisor to guide them to success?

- What if we gave every student a personal roadmap leading to their academic goals?

- What if each advisor was cross-trained to meet most of the student's needs?

- What if we connected it all through technology?

- What if we invented a new way of doing business and designed a facility to support it?

Plans for a new model of academic advising came at an opportune time since the college was also planning to renovate the student service facility. College leaders worked on a new model of academic advising at the same time they redesigned the existing facility to house the new model. While the primary focus for the program and facility redesign was on the main campus, the branch campuses also redesigned their student service facilities to complement the new model of academic advising. The model brought together all the services needed by students into a central location facilitated by an individual advisor assigned to each student as a single resource for the various services. Student services at every campus became the hub for easy access to resources and support staff. To make the new model work, all advisors were cross-trained in core concepts and core services.

ADVISOR AS PRIMARY CONTACT

Once a potential student applies for admission, he or she is notified by e-mail and letter of application status. This information can also be reviewed within the online student system, referred to as MyIRSC. This system provides online access to the students' academic records and other student services. Upon admission, students are mailed a welcome letter that includes contact information for their assigned advisor. Additionally, each advisor receives a weekly report of newly assigned students.

Students are encouraged to contact their advisors to set up a personal advising session to review goals and aspirations, prior academic history, college-level placement, and challenges the students may be facing. Advisors facilitate communication with their students using various synchronous and asynchronous methods, including e-mail, phone, instant messaging, and social media. Advisors also see students by appointment and on a walk-in basis. Goals of the first advising interaction include exploring and clarifying vocational and career goals, declaring an appropriate major based on those goals, and creating an IAP based on enrollment plans. By providing students with an IAP, advisors share with students the information necessary to stay on track toward degree completion. Additionally, advisors assist students in making the transition into the college environment by helping them become familiar with MyIRSC, the college website, IRSC's learning management system, and their college e-mail address.

To facilitate this proactive, ongoing communication between advisors and students throughout their tenure at the college, students are encouraged to use their advisors as the primary point of contact with the institution. This one-stop service allows the advisor to track the student's progress and follow-up on the student's behalf when needed if complex and nonroutine problems arise. Advisors also redirect students to other college services such as tutoring, the health and wellness center, and special community agencies, when needed. This centralized approach to academic advising places value on the interpersonal relationship developed between advisor and student. The college has established benchmarks toward degree completion at 25%, 50%, 75%, and 100% of courses needed, and advisors routinely contact students to review progress when students achieve these benchmarks. Each semester IRSC sends a formal notice to all students who reach the 75% or greater benchmark.

Helping Students Avoid Excess Hours

With the goal of minimizing enrollment in excess hours, the IAP includes prerequisite requirements for the desired degree at the student's declared transfer institution. Recent Florida legislation requires that students in attendance at a university who have exceeded 110% of their degree program pay an excess hour surcharge. This legislative change provides an incentive for students to consider progress toward degree completion and reinforces the importance of following their IAPs. Additionally, Title IV regulations have long limited to 150% of the program the hours that students may be covered for aid. This makes it critical that students create a plan early in their educational career so they are not faced with a loss of federal financial support. By providing them with an IAP, advisors give students the information necessary to register only for required courses and avoid excess hours, which reduces tuition and the time to degree. Committed to creating a superior teaching and learning environment with affordable access for all students, IRSC was ranked as the 10th most affordable 4-year college in the country on the U.S. Department of Education's 2012 College Affordability and Transparency List (http://collegecost.ed.gov/catc).

THE PLANNING PROCESS

The IAP is the result of collaboration between the student and advisor and encourages the student's active participation in his or her educational planning. The IAP maps out the student's academic career, term by term, forming a logical path to degree completion. It is then stored within the advising module of the college's student information system, also accessible to the student through MyIRSC. The IAP is a permanent and flexible record the advisor and student can access and modify as needed. Students import their IAPs into the online class schedule search when registering for classes. All available sections of classes in their plan are displayed, streamlining the online registration process. Online registration has increased by 10% as students follow their plans with increased confidence in their ability to select the correct courses. This has freed up advisor time for development of in-depth advising and meaningful follow-up with students who need more personal interaction and support.

In a time when advisors are asked to do more with less, IRSC uses technological solutions to increase students' access to information and facilitate interaction with advisors. Technology allows rudimentary tasks to be automated and lets advisors invest their time and efforts in more personal interactions with their students (Multari, 2004). According to Steele and Carter (2002), "providing consistent information is a necessary and important part of good academic advising, even if the message is repetitive and published in several locations."

IMPROVING EFFICIENCY

As caseloads grew, the need to determine each assigned student's enrollment status became more apparent. Advisors met several times in 2009 to discuss possible solutions to this challenge and the instructional advisement chair began working with IRSC enterprise systems to develop an automated process for determining a student's status and attaching that status to the student's advising record. Implemented in spring 2010, advisors can now see whether assigned students are actively enrolled, graduated, not enrolled for 2 years or more, reinstated after returning to school from a break in attendance, or graduated from one degree program but continuing their studies toward a new degree.

At the same time these enrollment status categories were implemented in the advising system, a process for creating individualized reports was also created. Advisors can request reports from their caseload using a variety of criteria. The reports include advising status codes, program objective codes, and details such as whether the student is enrolled during the current term. For example, an advisor may request a report that includes only those students assigned to them from August 2010 to the present who are on active status and who are nursing majors. Both the status codes and advising reports save time and provide more efficient management of large case loads.

As a result of suggestions from advisors, the student assignment screen now includes the student's high school graduation date, which assists in determining whether a dual-enrolled student has graduated. It also includes contact information so that advisors do not have to search for this information elsewhere in the system. One of the most recent enhancements to IRSC's student system was implemented in fall 2011 with the addition of assigned advisors' names displayed next to the students' names on instructors' Web-based class rosters. The advisor's name is linked to his or her e-mail address, making it easy for the faculty member to communicate with the advisor.

Advising staff are working on more efficient ways to monitor student progress. The instructional advisement chair and enterprise systems have been collaborating on an automated system of e-mail communications that will be sent to students at the end of each semester. The advising plan will be matched against the classes in which the student has been enrolled. Grades will be reviewed to determine whether the classes are appropriate for the student's major and whether they reflect successful completion of the classes. Based on the results of this review, a customized e-mail will be sent to students from their assigned advisor either congratulating them for continued progress toward their degree goals or encouraging them to meet with their advisor for additional consultation. This new system can now determine whether students are following their plans and successfully completing classes; advisors will not have to research this information manually and will have more time to spend advising students. Because of ongoing examination and assessment of this system's strengths and weaknesses, IRSC has been able to address and respond to advisors' concerns relatively quickly. This system is one of the keys to the successful expansion of IRSC's academic advising program.

NEW STUDENT ORIENTATION

Research shows that orientation services lead to higher student satisfaction, greater use of student support services, and improved retention of at-risk students. A national study by the Community College Survey of Student Engagement (CCCSE) showed, however, that after 3 weeks of college, 19% of entering students (14,416 of 74,261) were unaware of orientation offerings (CCSSE, 2012). As these findings were being published in spring 2012, IRSC was in the process of implementing an online new student orientation. NSO is a mandatory online noncredit course required of all first-time IRSC students, including dual-enrollment students. It contains a series of self-paced modules within the IRSC learning management system that require approximately 4–6 hours to complete. Module topics include financial literacy, student activities, library resources, and academic support services. Additional NSO requirements include completing an IAP with the assigned advisor, obtaining a student ID, activating a college e-mail account, and taking a learning styles assessment. All NSO modules and requirements must be completed prior to registration for any subsequent terms.

ADVISOR TRAINING

Prior to the first assignment of students to advisors in April 2007, advisors from all IRSC campuses participated in an intensive training program in the new advising system. The advising system allows for entry of advising plans through either of two options: a Web-based option accessed from within the IRSC employee website or through the student information system screens. Advisors were trained by the chair of instructional advisement in the use of both systems to allow for the flexibility of creating advising plans. Because a significant portion of the system was designed through a collaborative process that included advisors from all IRSC campuses, most advisors were already familiar with the screens and functions of the two approaches. Advisors also participated in the testing phase of the system and made valuable suggestions and comments that were incorporated into the final product. This participation resulted in the collective buy-in that allowed training to be collaborative and resulted in a much more enthusiastic adoption of the process.

Advisors from all five IRSC campuses met regularly prior to the implementation of the system to review screens, discuss concerns, and plan strategies. Under the direction of the chair of instructional advisement, these meetings are now scheduled at least once each semester. This ongoing solicitation of ideas and suggestions has resulted in a number of system enhancements that have benefited advising staff as well as other staff, faculty, and students.

When new advisors are hired, they are first trained in how to use the system, including an overview of navigational pointers for both the Web-based and mainframe options. A significant amount of time is also spent discussing effective caseload management. New advisors then spend at least one full week observing other advisors as they meet with students to develop advising plans. This week-long experience provides new advisors with the opportunity to observe different academic advising approaches and strategies used by seasoned advisors.

TECHNOLOGY INTEGRATION

Technology has played an integral part in implementing the academic advising program, particularly the individualized advising plan, which is the foundation for advising. Reports are available in the system to alert the advisor if a student is not following the IAP. For example, if a student's plan included nursing prerequisites but he or she registered for business courses, the advisor would know to touch base with the student to clarify new goals and adjust the plan.

IRSC is a member of the Higher Education Technology Group, which is a Florida-based consortium of colleges working together to develop and maintain a student information system that meets Florida state requirements while focusing on the unique needs of comprehensive state colleges. Member institutions within the consortium have access to source programming and may modify the software to suit an individual college's needs and business practices. To implement IAPs, IRSC reviewed and modified a component of the software relative to student academic planning. The final product was a Web-based system available to students and advisors. All plans are electronically housed in a central database allowing students to visit any campus to ask questions or seek advice. All members of the advising staff have access to students' IAPs to ensure that all who advise a student are offering consistent messages.

High school guidance counselors are given access to the IAP for dual-enrollment students. This adds another layer of value to the system by providing direct communication between the high school counselor and the college advisor. In compliance with FERPA guidelines, students provide IRSC with permission to share academic records with their parents and high school guidance counselors as part of the dual-enrollment application process. This shared advising system also notifies high school guidance counselors of registration changes and student withdrawals.

PROGRAM EVALUATION

The initial evaluation focused on the number of IAPs completed by each advisor. By identifying advisors who had higher IAP completion rates, colleagues could share best practices that could be used across the campuses. This was important information given that students were not required to complete an IAP prior to the implementation of the new student orientation. It also provided the information necessary for supervising administrators to make adjustments in business practices to support the initiative based on the needs of their advisors.

With completion of an IAP now a requirement for NSO, an increase in completion rates is anticipated. Because advisors will spend less time attempting to contact students in order to complete an IAP, they can focus more time on students who deviate from their plans or on early alerts that indicate students need help. As a result, advisors contact these at-risk students earlier in their academic careers and connect them with resources across campus, including additional career exploration and advisement, academic tutoring, and other support services. Along with completion of IAPs, evaluation will expand to include a more qualitative measurement of advising interactions with students and how those interactions promote retention and program completion.

An important outcome of having students assigned to advisors is the addition of the assigned advisor contact information to the faculty class roster. This created a direct link between the faculty and advisor, facilitating streamlined communication and providing a consistent and unified message between the institution and student. It has become a critical component of IRSC's ongoing emphasis on a more aggressive approach to early alert.

Graduation rates of students with and without IAPs were compared for two first-time-in-college (FTIC) cohorts (see Table 6.1). The graduation rate for students with IAPs for the fall 2008 cohort was approximately 54% higher than for those students without IAPs. For the fall 2009 cohort the graduation rate was 66% higher. Prior to the implementation of mandatory NSO in spring 2012, students were not required to meet with the assigned advisor to develop an IAP. As a result, not all students had IAPs. The higher graduation rates in these cohorts for students with IAPs supported the recently implemented requirement that all students meet with the assigned advisor to complete an IAP as part of new student orientation.

By tracking cohorts of FTIC students, we have found that students with advising plans have higher cumulative GPAs as well as higher persistence and retention rates. Eighty-seven percent of the FTIC students admitted in fall 2011 who had IAPs returned the following spring term, while only 76% of their cohort counterparts without IAPs returned. Similarly, FTIC students in the fall 2011 cohort who had IAPs had a cumulative GPA of 2.44 while those students without plans had a 2.13. While we cannot make causal claims, these findings support IRSC's primary goals for implementing IAPs. Table 6.2 summarizes GPAs as well as persistence and retention rates for FTIC students dating back to the fall 2008 cohort.

Table 6.1 ◆ Graduation Rates for First-Time-in-College Students at Indian River State College: 2008–2009

| Advising Plan | Fall 2008 | | | | Fall 2009 | | | |
| | Cohort | | Graduates | | Cohort | | Graduates | |
	#	%	#	%	#	%	#	%
With IAP	470	86.7%	111	23.6%	622	84.4%	99	15.9%
Without IAP	72	13.3%	11	15.3%	115	15.6%	11	9.6%
Total	542				737			

Table 6.2 ◆ GPAs and Persistence and Retention Rates for First-Time-in-College Students at Indian River State College: 2008–2011

Advising Plan	#	%	GPA	Persistence Returned spring #	Persistence Returned spring %	Retention Year 1 #	Retention Year 1 %	Retention Year 2 #	Retention Year 2 %
Fall 2008 Cohort									
With IAP	470	86.7%	2.31	384	87.1%	326	69.4%	306	65.1%
Without IAP	72	13.3%	1.95	45	62.5%	39	54.2%	36	50.0%
Total	542								
Fall 2009 Cohort									
With IAP	622	84.4%	2.15	507	81.5%	415	66.7%	388	62.4%
Without IAP	115	15.6%	1.90	81	70.4%	65	56.5%	62	53.9%
Total	737								
Fall 2010 Cohort									
With IAP	712	84.8%	2.23	596	83.7%	507	71.2%		
Without IAP	·128	15.2%	1.92	84	65.6%	61	47.7%		
Total	840								
Fall 2011 Cohort									
With IAP	655	73.7%	2.44	572	87.3%				
Without IAP	234	26.3%	2.13	178	76.1%				
Total	889								

A PERSONAL PERSPECTIVE

Research nationwide suggests that academic advising is one of the most important aspects of the educational experience (e.g., Noel-Levitz, 2009). The IAP is the key feature of IRSC's academic advising program and has played a major role in increasing students' confidence, motivating students to complete courses, and increasing communication between faculty members and advisors to foster student success, improved student retention and completion, and increased graduation rates. Potential challenges that other colleges may face when implementing IAPs include technical infrastructure limitations and student buy-in. Colleges need to carefully evaluate and assess their current technical infrastructure before implementing a similar program to ensure that the technology can support the practices.

It is also vital that information technology staff and academic advising professionals work together to create a student-friendly product. Students need to be trained in the use of the online registration system and using their IAPs as a course selection and registration resource. As a result of having access to information, students become more self-sufficient and empowered to take an active role in the decisions that affect their academic goals. This dynamic shifts the relationship between advisor and student to a partnership in which the student is more engaged and the advisor serves as both a mentor and teacher.

IRSC chose to begin advisor assignments from a specific date forward, assigning only first-time IRSC students during the implementation term. As a result, not all enrolled students have an assigned advisor. This decision assisted IRSC in keeping initial student caseloads manageable. Students who were not assigned an advisor could still request IAPs on a walk-in or appointment basis at their campus of choice. There are several places within the student information system that allow staff to view whether a student has an assigned advisor and, if so, the advisor's name. This search for advisor information is a routine part of the response to any student inquiry and serves to continually reinforce students' relationships with their assigned advisors.

Special institutional conditions must exist to support this program: a networked system that provides information to students and a cohesive, well-trained group of advisors who communicate well. The implementation of any new program or initiative requires a period of trial and error, so communication among advisors is critical to working out any problems in programming, delivery, or training. In a multi-campus or multi-college district, a networked system of well-trained advisors will ensure that students receive correct and consistent information at any campus from any advisor.

IRSC supports the national and state goals of the completion agenda and believes that its academic advising system is the key to meeting those goals. For institutions of higher education to produce more graduates, they must retain their students and increase student persistence (Milem & Berger, 1997; Tinto, 1975). Advisors have a positive impact on students' academic success, thereby playing a vital role in student retention (Dirr, 1999; Fishback, Kasworm, & Polson, 2002). Advisors familiar with the concept of developmental advising understand that relationship building is critical (Crockett, 1978).

Faculty members and administrators at IRSC recognize the success of the IAPs in supporting student retention and completion. They consistently applaud the collaboration fostered by listing the advisor's name on the class roster. Casey Lunceford, IRSC dean of arts and sciences stated,

> *We have a bachelor's degree in biology at IRSC. Many students try to manage their schedules and program from remote sites. The online individualized plan allows us to reach students and help them plan. The tremendous enrollment growth in our first twelve months of the program can be linked to strong academic advising and collaboration between our department and educational services. (personal communication)*

Leslie Kandefer, counselor at the Clark Advanced Learning Center charter high school values the program in assisting students with dual enrollment:

> *The plan helps students take ownership of their degree-seeking process. They can see a well-thought-out plan for reaching their goal and see how each course helps move them along. They can see the importance of doing well in every course to keep up the momentum. The online advising plans have also helped ensure that students get seats in classes by using the plan to search for courses that fit into their schedule; and they can do all this online. (personal communication)*

In our view, this program is exemplary and could be of use to other community colleges. We assign an individual advisor to our students for direction and encouragement throughout their academic tenure at IRSC. Students thrive in an environment where they feel supported and valued. Making academic advising a personal experience is one way we provide this support. Feedback from students has been excellent. In a letter expressing gratitude to her assigned advisor, one student wrote, "At our first meeting you provided a schedule that I should follow each semester. That schedule has kept me focused and it has also given me confidence." By making it personal, IRSC is beginning to hear similar messages from a great many of our students.

REFERENCES

Astin, A. W. (1984). Student involvement: A developmental theory for higher education. *Journal of College Student Personnel, 25*(4), 297–308.

Center for Community College Student Engagement. (2012). *A matter of degrees: Promising practices for community college student success.* Retrieved from http://www.ccsse.org/survey/survey.cfm

Crockett, D. S. (1978). Academic advising: A cornerstone of student retention. In L. Noel (Ed.), *Reducing the dropout rate* (pp. 29–35). San Francisco: Jossey-Bass.

Cuseo, J. (2003). *Academic advisement and student retention: Empirical connections and systemic interventions.* Brevard, NC: Policy Center on the First Year of College.

Dirr, P. J. (1999). *Putting principles into practice: Promoting effective student support services for students in online learning programs: A report on the findings of a survey.* Alexandria, VA: Public Service Telecommunications Corporation.

Ender, S. C., Winston, R. B., Jr., & Miller, T. K. (1982). Academic advising as student development. *New Directions for Student Services, 17,* 3–18.

Fishback, S. J., Kasworm, C. E., & Polson, C. J. (2002). *Responding to adult learners in higher education.* Melbourne, FL: Krieger Publishing Company.

Glennen, R. E. (1996). How advising and retention of students improves fiscal stability. *NACADA Journal, 16*(1), 38–46.

Habley, W. R. (2004). *The status of academic advising: Findings from the ACT Sixth National Survey* (NACADA Monograph Series No. 10). Manhattan, KS: National Academic Advising Association.

Metzner, B. S. (1989). Perceived quality of academic advising: The effect on freshman attrition. *American Educational Research Journal, 26*(3), 422–442.

Milem, J. F., & Berger, J. B. (1997). A modified model of student persistence: Exploring the relationship between Astin's theory of involvement and Tinto's theory of student departure. *Journal of College Student Development, 38*, 387–400.

Multari, R. J. (2004). Technology in higher education academic advisement. *The Mentor: An Academic Advising Journal.* Retrieved from http://dus.psu.edu/mentor/040107rm.htm

Noel, L. (Ed.). (1978). *Reducing the dropout rate.* San Francisco: Jossey-Bass.

Noel-Levitz, Inc. (2009). *2009 student satisfaction and priorities report.* Available from https://www.noellevitz.com/papers-research-higher-education/2009/1008

Pascarella, E. T., &Terenzini, P. T. (1991). *How college affects students: Findings from twenty years of research.* San Francisco: Jossey-Bass.

Ramist, L. (1981). *College student attrition and retention* (College Board Report No. 81-1). New York: College Entrance Board.

Steele, G., & Carter, A. (2002). Managing electronic communication technologies for more effective advising. *Academic Advising News, 25*(4). Retrieved from http://www.nacada.ksu.edu/Clearinghouse/AdvisingIssues/electronic.htm

Tinto, V. (1975). Dropout from higher education: A theoretical synthesis of recent research. *Review of Educational Research, 45*, 89–125.

Tinto, V. (1999). Taking retention seriously: Rethinking the first year of college. *NACADA Journal, 19*(2), 5–9.

CHAPTER 7

Community College of Baltimore County: An Achieving the Dream Model of Student Advising

Maureen O'Brien and Lillian Archer

The Community College of Baltimore County (CCBC), created in 1998 by the merger of three area community colleges, is now the largest provider of higher education and workforce development training in the Baltimore metropolitan area. With three main campuses and three extension centers, CCBC serves more than 71,000 students and offers more than 100 degrees, credit certificates, and career training licensure and certificates. CCBC is known for providing outstanding health-care profession training in the state, in both credit and noncredit course work. In 2011 the college was recognized by the *Chronicle of Higher Education* as "a great college to work for." CCBC's mission is to provide accessible, affordable, and high-quality education that prepares students for transfer and career success, strengthens the regional workforce, and enriches the community. CCBC became an Achieving the Dream (ATD) college in 2009. ATD is a long-term national initiative to help more community college students succeed—particularly those who traditionally face the most significant barriers to success. The initiative is built on the belief that broad institutional change, informed by student achievement data, is critical to significantly improving student success rates.

ADVISING HAD BEEN IDENTIFIED AS a key focus area for Community College of Baltimore County (CCBC) through its participation in the Achieving the Dream: Community Colleges Count (ATD) initiative. CCBC's current advisement model, created in 2010, is based on recommendations made by a CCBC advising task force in 2008. The task force recommended a shift from a prescriptive approach—where students take little responsibility for the academic planning process—to a developmental approach allowing students to be integral to the planning process and demonstrate self-direction and independent learning. For most of CCBC's history, the majority of students were advised by professional advisors in a centralized location. All new students were required to see an advisor for assessment, but there was no requirement for these new students to return for further advising following assessment. Continuing students came to advising on a rolling basis as soon as the semester course schedule was published, right up until and after classes began. With no deadline for registration, continuing students often waited until the rush of peak registration, arriving at the same time as new students. This created long wait times for students (60–90 minutes) and short meeting times with advisors.

During the summer registration period of 2009, there were more than 43,000 student contacts collegewide (April to September). At that same time, Community College Survey of Student Engagement (CCSSE) data showed that, while 93% of students were satisfied with advising services, the frequency of student contact with advising ranged from 56% to 59%. And despite the high level of satisfaction report, students did not typically follow through by coming to see an advisor; only slightly more than half of them actually returned to meet with an advisor beyond that first semester. When they did return, they came at peak times when the service was rushed, and their focus was on quick selection of courses for the impending semester rather than on long-term education planning.

Moreover, comments on CCBC's advising point-of-service survey indicated that students came to advising centers for information and services readily attainable on the website, such as viewing the class schedule or catalog, registering for classes, and seeking transfer information. Many survey comments pointed to a general lack of knowledge of what is expected of a college student. It was clear that the advising program was not meeting the needs of students, nor was it efficient or effective. The advising program formulated in 2010 incorporated some of the same foundational components of the 2008 task force report:

- The advising model must be dynamic and requires systematic review and evaluation.

- Personnel, space, technology, and equipment resources will be required to support the program.

- Students must be active partners in their education plans.

- Faculty will be incorporated into advising in a shared model. Use of both professional and faculty advisors "build on the strength of each" (King, 2002).

- Training will be integral and ongoing.

- In conjunction with advisors, students will create education plans that can be followed and modified each semester.

- Technology will be an essential component. All student systems must be user-friendly to support independent learning.

- Student learning outcomes will be incorporated for each stage of the plan.

CCBC began to examine other advising models with a review of NACADA literature and by attending regional and national seminars sponsored by the association. CCBC also had the support of the ATD collegewide committee that included key leaders from every department in the college. From reviewing the literature, participating in national seminars, and discussing with colleagues, CCBC agreed on the following priorities to frame the new academic advising program:

- Front-loading critical academic and career information for new students.

- Faculty advising for declared majors.

- Teaching students to be independent learners.

- Targeting academic action students (students on probation and suspension).

An advising syllabus was created that contained a mission statement, learning outcomes for students, and expectations for students and advisors. The mission statement included a commitment to engage students in meaningful partnerships to assist them in achieving education goals. It included support for exploration of programs of study, setting appropriate goals, and preparation for transfer or employment. A "stages of student learning" chart was adapted from a NACADA conference to demonstrate what students need to know—and when they need to know it—to be successful in college. The model has continued to evolve as CCBC implements components and evaluates them for inclusion in the program.

ORGANIZATION OF ACADEMIC ADVISEMENT

The academic advisement program emerged from the reorganization of CCBC enrollment management and learning and student development in 2007. Before the reorganization, a dean of students at each of the main campuses implemented different procedures and processes for advising. The reorganization created a centralized management team with one vice president of enrollment and student services (ESS) and three deans—one for student development, enrollment management, and college life.

The dean of student development oversees academic advising, career development, clinical counseling, disability support services, testing and assessment, and TRIO programs for the entire college. The director of advisement reports to the dean of student development and oversees the advising operations for CCBC's three main campuses and three extension centers. Four assistant directors manage advising on the three main campuses and one of the large extension centers. There are 24 full-time professional advisors. The full-time staff is augmented by 48 part-time professional advisors throughout the year, with increased hours at peak registration periods (23 FTE employees at peak and 11.6 FTE employees during nonpeak). In addition to the part-time advisors, advising centers hire student assistants during registration periods (April to August and November to January) to assist new and continuing students with registration.

Before ATD, the most extensive collaboration between ESS and the office of instruction involved developmental education policy and procedure implementation, and included a 2-year controlled study of learning communities with an external research organization, MDRC. A second and important collaboration between the enrollment and instruction offices began 2 years ago with the implementation of the academic advisement training modules for faculty. This included training for faculty teaching the new orientation course and for faculty who volunteered to advise students in their discipline specialty.

COMPONENTS OF THE ADVISING PROGRAM

Between 2008 and 2011, CCBC experienced an unprecedented enrollment surge of 36%. Also within that timeframe, the college became an ATD institution with academic advising identified as a key area for review and change. A comprehensive academic advising program was constructed to include early engagement of students. The program featured processes that assisted students in program planning that matched their abilities and interests, aided with decision making and goal setting, and taught students to use available technology. The program identified a clear mission for academic advising, created strong collaboration between student services and instruction, established clearly articulated procedures, formulated a comprehensive training plan for all professional advisors, and targeted specific populations of students for tailored support services.

CCBC reviewed numerous advising models and determined the "total intake model" (Gordon, Habley, & Grites, 2008) was the best fit for CCBC. Initial advising is done in a centralized advising center staffed by full- and part-time professional advisors. Once students declare a major, they are assigned to faculty advisors, although institutionalizing systemic faculty advising is in the pilot stage. The strength of the model is front-loading advisement to ensure that students make good initial choices in their academic careers and work with faculty who have expertise in the chosen majors and contacts in the job market or with transfer institutions. While the program was being formulated, CCBC established a one-credit academic development orientation course (ACDV 101) required of all students new to college. Course topics include academic planning and decision making, orientation to college policies and resources, career exploration, study skills, and an introduction to the technology skills necessary to be successful in college. Academic advising is embedded in the course and is provided by the ACDV instructor while students are enrolled in the class. After completing ACDV 101, students return to professional advisors for further advising assistance.

Professional advisors begin the advising process with new students by discussing advising basics such as assessment; components of a degree; developmental education and prerequisite sequences; college terminology; credit load; and how to balance college, work, and personal life. A handout that provides a visual and graphic statement on these key topics is distributed to each new student. In addition, they receive a new student packet that includes checklists for admission, financial aid, testing, advisement, registration, and payment. Other information in the packet includes keys to college success, top 10 reasons why students succeed, transferability of courses, the advising syllabus, a sample degree plan for an associate in general studies, enrollment services information, a FAFSA worksheet, and various flyers on services such as disability support and honors programs.

The advisor assists the student with creating a two-semester academic plan; a copy is given to the student for online registration, and another copy is scanned into the Banner student information system. This plan can be used by the student in the ACDV 101 class, in consultation with the instructor, to plan the second semester. In addition, the instructor can use the Banner graduation audit tool, CAPP, to help the student plan for subsequent semesters. Once the student declares a major, he or she is transitioned to a faculty advisor. A system of faculty advising is in the pilot stages at CCBC. Figure 7.1 depicts the advising experience of students who are new to CCBC.

DATA COLLECTION

It was clear from the beginning of the ESS reorganization that a comprehensive data collection system was necessary to inform decision-making about staffing and advising services. The scheduling and reporting system (SARS) was selected as the best tool to schedule students for a large, multicampus system and to provide data on students. SARS was launched in summer 2009 and proved helpful in making the case for additional full-time advisors and the continuing funding of part-time staff. Based on careful collection and use of data, CCBC has been able to double the

Figure 7.1 ◆ Flow of the Advising Experience for Students at Community College of Baltimore County

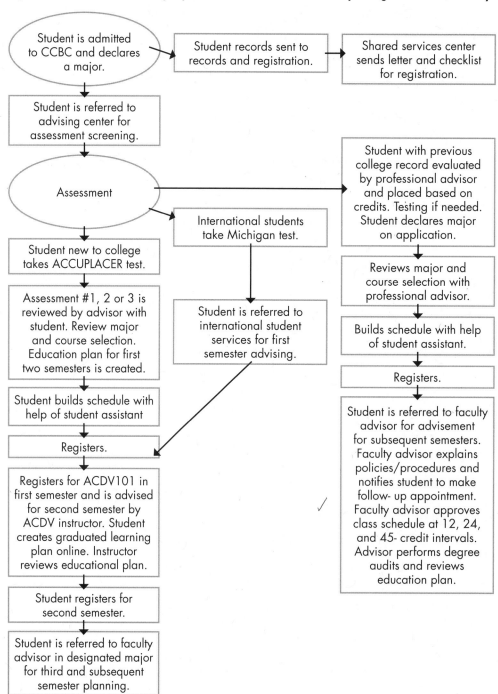

number of full-time staff since 2008 and has continued to garner temporary hourly salary dollars to support the operation, especially during peak registration. Other departments within enrollment and student services have begun to use SARS and have been trained by the advising SARS liaison who is a professional advisor. Moreover, advising has continued to expand its use of SARS using SARS-CALL for student messaging and eSARS as a way for students to make appointments online. SARSALRT will be implemented as part of an early alert system.

For most of the history of advising at CCBC, there was no way of documenting advising sessions other than with the paper files kept by individual advisors. The large number of student contacts at CCBC made it impractical to keep a record of every advising session, especially during peak times. In 2009, CCBC began using SPACMNT, the note function in the Banner system. Since that time, all advisors document all advising sessions with students. These accumulated records of advising sessions document the services of staff, especially the many part-time staff, and provide an accounting of decisions and recommendations made by advisors and students.

As part of the commitment to creating a culture of evidence prompted in part by involvement in ATD, CCBC examined success rates of students on academic probation or suspension (academic action). The intent was to determine the rate of return on investment given the enormous amount of staff time and resources necessary to address the needs of this population. Previously, students placed on academic probation were handled within academic advisement on a walk-in basis, rather than by appointment. Although students were notified of their academic standing as soon as grades were posted, and urged to send an appeal letter if they wanted to register for more than seven credits, they most frequently waited until the last minute to meet with advisors. In this situation, interactions with students were rushed, and approval processes for the appeals were inconsistent across the campuses. Some campuses provided nearly automatic approvals; others were more conservative in granting approval.

Students placed on academic suspension were notified to send a letter to one of the assistant directors of advising on one of the three main campuses if they wished to appeal to take classes in the following semester. Otherwise, they would be required to sit out for a full academic year, as stipulated in the academic action policy. Many hours were spent reviewing these letters and conducting hearings with all who appealed. Because of the extensive personnel time commitment to this special group of students, a committee was formed to study trends, practices, and related outcomes. The committee reviewed several semesters of data, which included a review of notes from advisors regarding student follow-up visits, grade point averages, registration patterns, and completion rates. In addition, the CCBC office of planning, research, and evaluation (PRE) conducted a study of academic action students. The study tracked students who were placed on academic action at the end of the fall 2007 semester to determine continuous enrollment patterns and academic progress as measured by GPA. By fall 2010, only 201 (18%) of the original 1,110 students were still enrolled.

In response to these data, the advising committee implemented procedural changes related to students on academic probation. Previously, students completed a "plan for success," a tool devised to focus them on the identification of areas that presented barriers to their success (time management, study skills, use of resources, motivation, goal setting, etc.). This often resulted in a rush to fill out the form, because students did not visit advisors until the most challenging time in terms of student volume (i.e., late in the registration period). The revised practice involves mailing the plan for success to students along with a notification letter and instructing students to contact advising offices for appointments with academic advisors. Students are instructed to come to the appointment with a completed plan to encourage them to review the conditions they perceive related to their poor academic performance.

The committee also reviewed national literature that suggested limiting students on probation to six or seven credits if they had previously taken a full-time load. Based on this information, a major change was instituted; now very few students on probation receive approval to take more than seven credits. In addition, each student is guided through a case management process with an assigned advisor.

Much like processes for students on academic probation, processes for academic suspension students have been evolving over the last 5 years as well. The practice had been to readmit most suspended students who wrote an appeal letter and to allow them to reenroll for a full-time load of 12 credits. In the new approach, each suspended student must participate in a hearing board made up of cross-functional representatives including advising and career counseling. CCBC's guidelines regarding conditions required for readmission are now collegewide to prevent students from shopping around for readmission decisions. Despite these efforts, a review of return rates, GPA, and registration patterns showed that many academically suspended students who appealed and were reinstated did not return for the subsequent semester.

Staff members were devoting more than 3,700 hours per year to this process and yet many students still did not return or, if they did return, they eventually dropped out. As a result, CCBC championed a change to the suspension policy, dropping the appeal process, as we believed the probation process offered students many semesters of intervention opportunities. Passed by the college senate and approved by CCBC senior staff, the policy went into effect July 1, 2012. With approval of the new policy, students will no longer have the option of appeal following academic suspension. Rather, they will be required to sit out for a full academic year.

FACULTY ADVISING

CCBC has a rich tradition of faculty advising, but it has not been systemic, and common standards have been lacking across the colleges. In 2002, a task force was charged with creating a faculty advising model, and while many good ideas were generated and vetted, the final work of the task force was not adopted due to faculty contract issues such as workload and associated compensation. In 2008, CCBC piloted a new faculty advising model in which approximately 30 faculty from various disciplines volunteered and were trained by advisors. In this pilot, students in a variety of majors were assigned to these trained faculty members, although students were not systematically matched to the faculty member's area of disciplinary expertise. This pilot of a new model proved to be unsuccessful for faculty and students.

When advising became a priority of the ATD initiative for the college, a sub-group of the ATD planning team decided on a different approach for the next faculty advising pilot effort. This time, faculty would advise students who had declared a major in the subject matter taught by that faculty member. Two majors in each of the six CCBC schools—for a total of 12 majors—were selected for the pilot. The new pilot called for faculty to advise students who had accrued 40+ credits in their major. The CCBC registrar's office identified about 600 students for this cohort, and the pilot was launched in fall 2011. Approximately 30 faculty members were trained by professional advisors in 2-day training sessions for 2.5 hours each day. This pilot is ongoing, and additional programs are being carefully selected and added as we continue to explore how best to use faculty advisors to increase student success. *Work in process*

ADVISOR TRAINING

Ongoing training and professional development are necessary and critical components of any high-quality, comprehensive academic advising program. Also critical is the assessment of the advising program and individual advisors and recognition and rewards for those who deliver academic advising (Gordon, Habley, & Grites, 2008). Comprehensive advisor training and development should be an intentional, ongoing process. This process must support advisors in the acquisition of the perspectives and tools needed to expand their knowledge, understanding, and skills to enhance student learning, engagement, and success (Brown, 2008). Additionally, training and development should be focused on the specific needs of all who provide advisement (new, seasoned, full- and part-time professional advisors, faculty, and student services staff) and tailored to the specific learning outcomes necessary for each population.

Although content and desired learning outcomes of advisor training programs may vary according to the needs of different populations, all training and development should be structured around three common elements: conceptual, relational, and informational as proposed by leading experts in academic advising. Each element should be addressed equally. All too often, advisor training skews heavily toward informational content to the exclusion of the other key elements (see Table 7.1).

The conceptual component of an advisor training program focuses on what advisors need to understand about the students they serve, as well as the guiding principles of the profession. This training component should include information related to student development theory, the NACADA core concepts and mission, the teaching-learning nature of the advising relationship, and ethics. Due to the ever-changing nature of institutional policies, procedures, programs, and resources, ongoing training related to the informational aspect of advising work is particularly important. This component of advisor training focuses on establishing and updating a common repository of knowledge related to academic programs, policies, and procedures that affect the development of education plans for students.

Table 7.1 ◆ Sample Advisor Training Learning Outcomes

| | Learning Outcomes | |
Conceptual	Informational	Relational
New Advisors		
Advisors will understand the concept of advising as teaching/learning.	Advisors will know and understand general education requirements.	Advisors will appreciate cultural differences.
Advisors will understand the core values of advising.	Advisors will understand FERPA.	Advisors will understand the boundaries of academic advising and personal counseling.
Advisors will be familiar with student development theory.	Advisors will be able to document sessions with appropriate SPACMNT notes.	Advisors will respect and value students.
Advisor Level 1		
Advisors will develop a plan to apply the conceptual framework covered in new advisor training to daily practice.	Advisors will be knowledgeable about transfer issues.	Advisors will demonstrate effective conflict resolution skills.
Advisors will comprehend the relationship of career counseling to academic advising.	Advisors will be able to identify career options for all academic programs.	Advisors will demonstrate the use of professional judgment.
Advisors will discern and appreciate learning styles.	Advisors will understand the financial aid process.	Advisors will develop a plan to collaborate with faculty.

The relational component deals with the skills advisors need to effectively communicate essential information to students. This component involves areas such as "relationship building, communication skills, questioning skills, and mentoring skills" (Drake, 2007). Also included are "skills and attitudes that advisors need to engage students in goal setting, academic planning, and decision making" (Spence, 2010). Time spent on this component is crucial to the quality of communication necessary to achieve the desired learning outcomes of the advisor–advisee partnership.

Launched in 2010, the new model of advisor training based on the core components (conceptual, informational, and relational) focused on ongoing, mandatory, systematic, year-round advisor training and development designed to advance progressively the skills of all who advise. Specific learning outcomes were identified and are assessed for each of the three stages of the progressive training process. Each stage requires 12 hours of training. New professional advisors—full and part-time—advance through progressive training levels for one year. Each training level focuses on specific content with particular areas of concentration. They are described as follows:

- New Advisor Training: Upon successful completion of the initial module (including the assessment of specific learning outcomes), which focuses on basic information that new advisors need to know to begin advising students who are new to the college, participants begin to shadow experienced advisors. After a designated period of time, new advisors can begin to work with students under the supervision of a mentor.

- New Advisor Training Level 1: Advisors who have successfully completed new advisor training and have begun to work with students are required to complete the second module within the first semester they begin advising. More in-depth information regarding majors, transfer, and college resources is introduced. Learning outcomes are developed and tailored to the needs of advisors relatively new to the profession and who have begun to work with students. The goal is to expand the breadth and depth of the new advisor's conceptual, informational, and relational knowledge.

- New Advisor Training Level 2: In their second semester, first-year advisors participate in the final level of formal training. This level is designed to advance the breadth and depth of their conceptual, informational, and relational understanding of the advisement process. During this level of training, advisors are introduced to more advanced techniques for working with at-risk students and students whose behavior requires intervention. At this level, there is also more immersion in transfer matters. Upon successful completion of this module, formal advisor training is concluded.

All advisors are required to provide evidence of participation in ongoing professional development activities related to maintenance and expansion of their conceptual, informational, and relational knowledge of the advising profession. Experienced professional advisors, upon completion of new advisor training, as well as levels 1 and 2, engage in year-round professional development opportunities, related but not restricted to the following:

- Regional and national NACADA conferences and meetings.

- Statewide advisor affinity meetings.

- Related conferences sponsored by other professional organizations (e.g., American Association of Community Colleges, League for Innovation in the Community College).

- Webinars.

As mentioned in the preceding section on faculty advising, a second faculty advising pilot was implemented in fall 2011. The initiation of this pilot created a need to modify and adapt the professional advisor training model to the needs of faculty advisors. Faculty involved in this advising pilot had needs that differed from new professional academic advisors; faculty were already well versed in their disciplines and the course requirements for their majors, and they would not be advising students from developmental course levels. Faculty were assigned to advise students from their own disciplines who would have accumulated 40 or more credits at the time of contact. Additionally, a faculty survey indicated that this group was not interested in the conceptual and relational aspects of academic advising; instead, they were more interested in basic information related to the technology involved in the advising process and information about transfer.

The training included an overview of academic advising, college policies and procedures, assessment, FERPA, transfer, use of technology, and support and referral services. A Blackboard training course had previously been established for professional advisor training and a faculty module was added. The participating faculty advisors rated the training as very good to excellent. Professional advisors continued to act as mentors for faculty. At the close of the pilot, about 200 students were advised by the trained faculty. A review of SPACMNT entries (electronic notes) showed that fewer than 30% of the sessions had been documented by the faculty advisors in Banner. A survey of the faculty participants revealed that many did not feel comfortable using the information screens in Banner.

Consequently, advisors modified faculty training to include more hands-on experience and opportunities to discuss advising scenarios. All faculty members participating in advising were required to attend refresher training in March 2012. A second cohort of students will be identified and two more majors have been added to the program. If this change is successful, CCBC will continue to add faculty and majors and increase the registration holds to another level of 24 credits.

EFFICACY OF CCBC'S ADVISING PROGRAM

There are several components of the advising program at CCBC that make it particularly effective and efficient for both students and staff. The first involves a multidepartmental triage process, designed and implemented to relieve the academic advising unit of the sole responsibility (and the student volume associated with it) for screening students prior to testing and advising. Several departments within ESS are involved in the process, allowing for effective use of staffing when needed most. The career services staff—separate from advising—assist with the important task of screening new students for assessment. This allows advisors one-on-one time with students who have completed testing and are ready to register, as well as more time with continuing students in the advising computer labs.

CCBC has used part-time staff in an efficient way by increasing their work hours during peak registration and reducing their work hours in nonpeak periods.

Part-time staff understand this arrangement when they are hired. CCBC keeps part-time staff employed throughout the year to keep up with all the details of advising services. Student helpers are hired only for peak registration, during which they assist both new and continuing students with registration in the labs. They also assist at the reception desks and triage stations throughout the college.

Technology is the second component that makes the program efficient and effective. Technology is used to lessen wait time for students and to teach them how to access the information they need. The SARS system allows tracking of student contacts, schedule staff, remind students of appointments via an automatic calling feature, and make electronic appointments with students. The system eventually will offer an early alert component.

CCBC's SharePoint site houses all policies, procedures, course information, and referral services for the college so anyone who advises may locate updates and information needed to work with students. All advisors are given access to the note function in Banner to document all advising sessions, which is critical for a multicampus institution where students may attend classes at two or more campuses and extension centers in one semester. When the department was reorganized, CCBC made it a priority to institute the same processes and procedures for all campuses and extension centers, ensuring that students could work with staff at any campus and receive the same information and service.

The advising training program is the third component that makes the CCBC program effective. It offers a two-tiered approach to professional advisor training and has integrated a training program for faculty advisors. It includes year-round, in-person workshops, training workshops on Blackboard, and handbooks for faculty. The program is organized in modules; advisors who complete the program are certified.

The fourth component is advising labs that are instituted during peak registration periods. These labs increase the number of students who can be advised by staff and offer students experience in the use of college and articulation information systems. Advisors and student assistants work with up to 20 students at a time in the labs, freeing other advisors to see new students individually. All of these features emerged from CCBC's review of data on programs and students, an examination of innovative programs, and discussions about how to make the advising centers more responsive to student needs in a period of unprecedented enrollment and reduced budgets.

USE OF TECHNOLOGY

With the enrollment surge that occurred between 2008 and 2011, it was apparent that advisement services would need to use technology more effectively to provide timely services to students. Several years prior, CCBC began using its Intranet to store college policies and procedures and referral information. Currently, CCBC uses SharePoint site to store all basic information that advisors need. The site houses information on advising and support services contacts, advising updates, staff documents, links to articulation and transfer sites, scholarship information, and a calendar of events. Two advisors keep the site updated weekly.

CCBC has offered online advising since 2004. Four advisors (three part-time) communicate with students electronically, answering general questions regarding CCBC and programs of study. In 2011, the online advisors served more than 2,300 student contacts, responding to each inquiry within 24 hours (during the work week). The full-time advisor who offers online advising also works on the advising Web and portal pages, in addition to providing technical support for online advising services.

An "Ask an Advisor" service is available through a form on the advising Web page. Students generally receive responses within one business day. This service is useful for students with general, policy-related questions as well as for students who are unable to visit the college for various reasons. Three main goals of online advising at CCBC are to

◆ Ensure that all communications comply with FERPA regulations.

◆ Teach students to be more self-sufficient and self-directed in their approaches to information exploration in college.

◆ Encourage students to meet with advisors in person, if possible, for specific questions that cannot be answered online.

Online advisors have created a large library of information in PDF form, providing directions for the student online information system as well as referrals to the college catalog for policies and course and program requirements. Online advising is an integral part of CCBC's program, and, as technology advances, CCBC expects that the way it interacts with students will evolve as well, keeping in mind the limitations of information disclosure and the overall mission of the college.

Much of the information on CCBC's Web pages will migrate to the new advising portal once it has been established. A committee of advisors worked on the portal site for approximately one year and presented a storyboard to the college portal committee in fall 2011. In keeping with collegewide committee suggestions, continuing education courses were embedded into the advising pages to provide information to all students, regardless of credit status. In addition, CCBC minimized college jargon on the site and added language more appropriate for students. Tabs reflect the questions students commonly have. "How do I choose classes?" "When do I see an advisor?" "Am I ready to graduate?"

The portal pages were modeled on the student learning chart that was part of the original comprehensive advising program. The chart details the different stages through which students migrate—from preenrollment to graduation—emphasizing completion. Once the portal pages are uploaded, students will be referred to this site by their orientation course instructors as well as professional and faculty advisors.

Students do not always take advantage of the information available to them on the CCBC website. The advising labs were established to teach students how to use the technology to access information to answer their questions. Most current students are comfortable with using technology tools because of the practice they receive in ACDV 101 classes. SARS is the storage site for advising calendars and data collection. It is used for automated calling when students need reminders and will be used for electronic appointments and for the early alert program.

The degree audit program of the Banner system, CAPP, has been used by advisors and the registrar's staff for about 6 years. Due to concerns about this system's user-friendliness, CCBC has purchased DegreeWorks, which is Banner-compatible and will be a better education planning tool to be used by both staff and students. A DegreeWorks team consisting of registrar, advising, and information technology staff is in place to work on templates and programs of study for this effort. Once

DegreeWorks is in place in 2013, it will also be used in the ACDV courses as the degree audit and planning instrument, replacing an in-house instrument that does not work well for students.

EXTERNAL FUNDING

In 2011, CCBC was awarded a $1.9 million U.S. Department of Education Title III Strengthening Institutions Program grant titled "Building a Culture of Success: Increasing Persistence, Retention, and Graduation." The project supports the comprehensive advising program, the developmental education program, and the one-stop service coordinated by enrollment services. This grant undergirds programs that have been in the planning stages within the ATD initiative and will allow the college to move forward quickly in implementing the DegreeWorks project.

EVALUATION

Evaluation of services and programs has played an integral part in all decisions and program modifications made in advising services. Decision making based on sound information has been a hallmark of CCBC's ATD experience. Advising has partnered with the office of planning, research, and evaluation from the beginning of the ATD project. All surveys and evaluations have been created in conjunction with the expertise of PRE staff. Advising uses a point-of-service survey and an advising lab survey, both of which are offered year-round.

Data are collected by PRE and sent to the director of advising for discussion with the advising and enrollment and student services leadership team. PRE assisted advising in the original evaluation of the pilot for the advising labs, which took place at two large campuses at CCBC for 6 weeks in summer 2010. Armed with the student evaluations of the labs and the numbers seen during that time period, CCBC was able to make the case for permanent labs adjacent to the advising centers at these campuses.

The labs were created during the fall semester of 2010 and were in operation by November 2010. More than 16,900 students have visited the labs since their inception, and the evaluations continue to be excellent. All students complete an online evaluation prior to exiting the labs. Evaluations in 2010 and 2011 indicated that 92% of students thought that the information they received was "helpful" or "very helpful." Ninety-four percent of the students visited the labs for "general advising" or "transfer information," and 89% indicated that they received all of the information they needed. Students requiring more extensive assistance, such as detailed discussion involving transfer choices, conversations involving success strategies, or anything of a personal nature, are referred to advisors for a one-to-one session.

CCBC also evaluated advising services through the use of focus groups. Group leaders were trained by a nationally known expert in the use of these groups. Three rounds of student focus groups were held. Answers to the focus group questions provided the college with information about how students viewed services from faculty, staff, and administrators in the intake process and the college environment in general. Issues were identified in testing, advising, financial aid, payment process, instructors, class cancellations, parking, and socializing. Students also stated they experienced problems related to transportation to college, college preparedness, balancing school and life, time management, and motivation. Advising staff summarized the results of the focus groups and used the information to improve many components of the advising program.

The advising management team also worked with PRE to evaluate "Advising Basics," a new initiative for incoming students. A written handout of the program titled "First Advising" introduces students to processes of assessment, advisement, and registration. CCBC wanted to determine whether the handout offered the kind of information students needed to get started in the college process. PRE assisted in designing an instrument to assess what students learned from the handout and their discussions with an advisor. A one-page survey included questions about testing, prerequisites, programs of study, and how to balance school and personal time; differences among students enrolled part-time and full-time were also explored. Students were asked to complete this quick questionnaire at the end of the advising session using the handout to answer the questions. It took them only 1–2 minutes to complete. The results showed that a majority of students understood the handout and discussion with the advisor, regardless of reading ability. Based on these results, CCBC now uses this handout with all new students at all campuses. It provides a structured approach for all advisors for the first advising conversations with students.

CONCLUSION

The advising program at CCBC works for a number of reasons, and components of it could work at other community colleges. Regardless of institutional size, location, or resources, applying these three lessons could improve any college's advising outcomes.

- Establish strong, team-based partnerships collegewide with key academic and support service areas, including instruction, information technology, and planning and research. Such cross-functional teamwork in the development, implementation, and evaluation of your advising program will ensure the top-down and lateral buy-in necessary to foster innovation and continuous improvement.

- Be data-driven and tech-savvy in your approach. This gives you an opportunity to pilot programs, evaluate them, fully implement or modify them in ways that truly advance best practices, and have the broadest possible impact by leveraging available technology.

- You can have collegewide buy-in, make decisions informed by data, and use the latest technology tools, but if you do not engage students in the process, advising may still fall short. Students need to be active participants in the advising process, willing and able to access the systems, resources, and tools in place to support them as independent learners. They need to understand what is required to be successful, develop realistic education and career goals, and accept responsibility for decisions made.

At CCBC, we make it very clear that we expect our students to use college resources, develop an education plan, articulate program requirements, and evaluate their progress to degree attainment. The advising computer labs continue the learning process by helping students explore education information on their own. The portal site will offer students a learning matrix, detailing what they need to know at each stage of their progression through their programs of study. The implementation of DegreeWorks will allow students to use the education plan to map out each semester, progressing toward graduation. Being team-based, data-driven, tech-supported, and student-led may not be the only considerations, but based on our experiences, they are essential to engaging students for success.

REFERENCES

Brown, T. E. (2008). Critical concepts in advisor training and development. In V. N. Gordon, W. R. Habley, T. J. Grites, & Associates (Eds.), *Academic advising: A comprehensive handbook* (2nd ed.). San Francisco: Jossey-Bass.

Chronicle of Higher Education. (2011). *Great colleges to work for 2011.* Available from http://chronicle.com/article/Great-Colleges-to-Work-For/128312/

Community College of Baltimore County. (2008). *Academic advising task force report.* Baltimore, MD: Author.

Drake, J. (2007). *Components of a successful faculty advising program* [Brochure]. Manhattan, KS: NACADA.

Gordon, V. N., Habley, W. R., Grites, T. J., & Associates. (Eds). (2008). *Academic advising: A comprehensive handbook* (2nd ed.). San Francisco: Jossey-Bass.

Habley, W. R. (2008). *Training, assessment, recognition and reward.* In V. N. Gordon, W. R.

Habley, T. J. Grites, & Associates (Eds.), *Academic advising: A comprehensive handbook* (2nd ed.). San Francisco: Jossey-Bass.

King, M. C. (2000). Designing effective training for academic advisors. In V. N. Gordon, W. R. Habley, & Associates (Eds.), *Academic advising: A comprehensive handbook* (pp. 289-297). San Francisco: Jossey-Bass.

King, M. C. (2002). *Community college advising.* Retrieved from http://www.nacada.ksu.edu/Resources/Clearinghouse/View-Articles/Two-year-college-advising.aspx

Spence, J. (2010). Developing and administering advisor training and development programs. In *Administrator's Institute session guide.* Manhattan, KS: NACADA.

ABOUT THE CONTRIBUTORS

S. Renea Akin is the associate vice president of learning initiatives at West Kentucky Community and Technical College, where she has been responsible for institutional planning, research, and effectiveness since 2007. Akin completed her doctorate in higher education leadership policy at Peabody College of Vanderbilt University. With 20 years of experience in the community college setting, Akin has presented at numerous conferences for community college audiences, primarily on the topics of accreditation and cultural transformation.

Sherry Anderson has worked at West Kentucky Community and Technical College for over 33 years. During that time she has served as a faculty member and business program coordinator, accreditation liaison, institutional effectiveness director, and dean of academic affairs. Currently, Anderson serves as the vice president of learning initiatives with oversight responsibility for online learning, institutional effectiveness and research, enrollment management, information technology, and special projects.

Lillian Archer is the dean of student development at the Community College of Baltimore County (CCBC) in Maryland. Before assuming her current role as dean, Lillian held multiple other leadership positions at CCBC including project director, director of counseling, and campus dean. Archer served as a commissioner on the Baltimore County Commission for Women and as an evaluator for the Academic Quality Improvement Program of the Higher Learning Commission. She holds an EdD in higher education with a concentration in community college leadership from Morgan State University (2002). In addition, Archer is a graduate of the American Council on Education Fellows Program, class of 2003–2004.

Meredith Coughlin provides academic advising services in her role as faculty counselor at the St. Lucie West Campus of Indian River State College (Florida). Actively involved in various institutional initiatives, Coughlin serves on the Academic Support and Success Workgroup and Distance Learning Enhancement Workgroup. Coughlin recently became learning styles–certified by the International Learning Styles Network and serves on the Learning Styles Committee focused on integrating learning styles into instructional experiences and academic advising services. She is also the lead advisor for the Nu Iota chapter of Phi Theta Kappa honor society. Coughlin is currently completing her doctoral research on integrating technology into quality academic advising at the University of Florida. She recently presented a co-authored paper about challenges faced by online doctoral students at the American Educational Research Association's 2012 annual conference in Vancouver, British Columbia, as well as a concurrent session focused on social media in academic advising at the Student Development Commission of the Association of Florida Colleges' 2012 annual meeting.

Dale Hayes chairs the Department of Instructional Advisement at Indian River State College (Florida). She has over 32 years of student services experience, including experience in student advisement, financial aid, and career and transition services. In addition, she has been instrumentally involved in the development of the student information system in use at IRSC and seven other colleges. She serves on several faculty committees, including the IRSC Curriculum Committee, and currently chairs the IRSC Scholarship and Loan Committee. Hayes has been a presenter at a number of student development conferences and was a finalist for the 2011 Association of Florida Colleges Exemplary Practice Award. She was also the recipient of the 2010 Student Development Advancement Award presented by the Student Development Commission of the Association of Florida Colleges. Hayes was selected by her faculty peers to receive the Anne R. Snyder Department Chair Excellence Award in 2009.

Joan L. Kindle is associate provost at William Rainey Harper College in Illinois. She has over 25 years of experience in community college leadership serving as assistant to the president, vice president of student affairs, and dean of student development. Kindle is an experienced presenter at professional association meetings including those of NASPA, the American Association of Community Colleges, and Achieving the Dream and has been recognized by NASPA as a Community College Outstanding Professional in her region and a national distinction as Pillar of the Profession.

Terry O'Banion is the president emeritus of the League for Innovation; since his retirement he has worked with the Bill and Melinda Gates Foundation, the MetLife

Foundation, Walden University, and The Chauncey Group International and currently serves full time as a distinguished professor and chair of the graduate faculty of National American University. In his 52 years in the community college arena, he has consulted in over 800 community colleges and has authored 15 books and over 190 articles, chapters, and reports. Five national awards have been established in his name. Contact O'Banion at obanion@league.org.

Maureen O'Brien began her career as a counselor (assistant professor) at the Community College of Baltimore County (CCBC) in Maryland in 1977. After attaining a master's in counseling psychology from Towson State College (Towson University), she was promoted to the rank of instructor and later to associate professor. Throughout her career at CCBC, O'Brien served in a number of leadership positions that included coordinator of Turning Point, a grant-funded program for displaced homemakers, and director of development, institutional advancement. In 1997, O'Brien returned to the counseling and advising department to serve as department chair and transfer coordinator. O'Brien served on the Faculty Senate and Academic Council for many years and as Chair of the Senate Budget committee. She punctuated her professional achievements in 2007 when she was selected to serve as director of academic advisement. She led with administrative prowess until her retirement in April 2012.

Angela Oriano is the associate director for college relations at the Center for Community College Student Engagement, an initiative of the Community College Leadership Program at The University of Texas at Austin, where she also serves as a lecturer in the Department of Educational Administration. Angela coordinated the development of the Center's Survey of Entering Student Engagement (SENSE), the Center's second national student survey. She has also served as a grant writer for Austin Community College in Texas and as the director of developmental education at Southeastern Community College (Iowa) where she helped lead the college's tutoring, supplemental instruction, and disability support services; managed the college's literacy, adult basic education, and corrections education programs; and served as an adjunct faculty member. Oriano is a frequent presenter and keynote speaker at national conferences and often facilitates workshops for colleges interested in using data to further their student success agendas. She is the board president of the Manengouba Foundation, an organization devoted to improving educational opportunities and outcomes for students in Cameroon, Africa, and is a member of one of the implementation teams for the 21st-Century Commission on the Future of Community Colleges.

Sheryl M. Otto is the assistant provost and dean of student development at William Rainey Harper College in Illinois. During her 21 years at Harper College she has provided leadership on a variety of initiatives including early alert, transfer articulation, outcomes assessment, program review, ERP (enterprise resource planning) implementation, and retention-based programming. She serves on the Illinois Articulation Initiative Advisory Council, is a former NASPA IV-East Regional Board member, and holds membership in several professional associations. In 2009 she was honored with the NASPA IV-East Distinguished Service to the Profession Award. She has presented at numerous regional and national conferences.

Steven Payne has worked in higher education since 1983, beginning his career as the director of financial aid at Lake Area Vocational Technical Institute (South Dakota). Later moving to Manchester College in Indiana (now Manchester University), he continued in financial aid as well as serving as the director of information technology. In 1999, he began his tenure at Indian River State College (IRSC) in Florida as the director of financial aid and then was appointed as the assistant dean of educational services in 2003. In this position, he is responsible for admissions, records, financial aid, testing, instructional advisement, and student success services. He holds a BA in sociology from Greenville College, Illinois, and an MA from the University of Illinois at Springfield in human development and counseling.

Joyce C. Romano is the vice president for student affairs at Valencia College in Florida. She has 30+ years of experience in residence life, student activities, and student services at community colleges and four year colleges and universities. Her work at Valencia has focused on the design and implementation of LifeMap, a developmental advising model and system; Atlas, an online portal learning community; and the redesign of student services with a focus on student learning of educational processes to support college completion. She co-led the Achieving the Dream initiative at Valencia, which focused on strategies to close the achievement gaps among students of color, underprepared students, and students from low-income families.

Eric Rosenthal is currently the director of academic advising and counseling at William Rainey Harper College in Illinois. He has spent his 18-year career in student affairs providing and directing student counseling and advising services. Rosenthal has written scholarly publications including a depiction of Harper College's counselor training program, which was featured in a NACADA advising administration monograph recognizing exemplary practices, and a journal article based on his doctoral dissertation on date rape prevention. Rosenthal has taught various undergraduate and graduate courses and has presented at several local, regional, and national conferences on diverse topics. He also enjoys presenting workshops for students and colleagues and facilitates a monthly stress management breakout session for unemployed community members as part of Harper College's Career Stimulus program. He is a member of NASPA and NACADA.

Deborah Smith serves as the director of advising and assessment services at West Kentucky Community and Technical College. Smith has 28 years of experience in higher education. Prior to accepting her current position, Smith served as a professor and program coordinator of radiography and as dean of the Allied Health and Personal Services division. Smith has conducted research and presented nationally on the benefits of pre-placement assessment advising.

Sandra Tucker currently serves as the director of online student services at West Kentucky Community and Technical College. She has 27 years of experience in student affairs, having held positions such as dean of students, registrar, and academic advisor. Tucker is a member of NACADA and KACADA and previously served on the executive board of KACRAO. She served on the Kentucky Council on Postsecondary General Education Communications Workgroup in 2010.

INDEX